WHY LEADERS QUIT

And How YOU Can Go the Distance

By Rev. Trisha R. Peach

Table of Contents

THE BUZZ

Here is what a few key ministry influencers are saying about <u>Why We Quit</u>.

The best way to be successful in ministry is to stay in ministry. But that's harder said than done. It takes wisdom, tenacity and a close walk with God to go the distance. Starting out many people don't understand just how challenging it is to go the distance. We know this by the reports we hear about the many leaders who step out of ministry each month. But it doesn't have to be that way. In this book, by my friend Trisha, you'll discover the keys and tools you need to stay faithful for life. This book can help you say what the Apostle Paul said at the end of his journey. He was able say "I have fought the good fight, I have finished the race and I have remained faithful." I believe greatness in ministry is not measured in years, but in decades. May that be our testimony.
Dale Hudson, Founder and CEO of Building Children's Ministry

Trisha Peach tackles one of the most pressing issues facing the Church, today. Ministerial burnout is a real crisis and affects the entire congregation, not just the pastor. In this book, Trisha informs, encourages, and empowers ministers to stay in it for the long haul. I pray you are inspired as you read and that you DON'T QUIT!
Brian Dollar
Author, Pastor, Founder of High Voltage Kids Ministry Resources
www.highvoltagekids.com

The Kingdom of God is transformed people who transform society. The evidence, however, seems to suggest that personal transformation and self-care is the one thing that consistently gets squeezed out of the calendar when the mission and the demands of church and church culture as it stands, come calling. This book is a call back to what is important. A reminder not to dismiss our own overburdened life as simply a season, but to address wholeness and health as a not just as a factor in good ministry but a fundamental foundation. Scripture says we can do nothing of our own strength, but all the strength we need is available to us as we abide in the vine. Thank you, Trisha, for reminding us what is at stake and daring to suggest a re-evaluation of what it truly means for a leader to be in Christ.

Nicki Straza
Discipleship/Leadership Development Pastor
Freedom House

If you've ever felt like quitting the ministry life, and I believe we all have at some point or another, then this book is for you! Trisha has done some wonderful research on this subject and my eyes were definitely opened. Too many times we choose to throw in the towel and give up because this is not what we signed up for. Ministry isn't supposed to be this hard. Trisha will help you see the warning signs of burnout and will give you guidance through the storms of ministry life. I believe you will also be encouraged by the real-life ministry stories she shares. What hope it brings to know we are not alone in serving the Lord in the ministry.

Vanessa Myers, Children's Minister, Author of Rise Up: Choosing Faith over Fear in Christian Ministry

I have admired Trisha Peach since the first time we sat down and talked. She is the real deal who loves God's people and the local church. I am so thankful I never quit in ministry to kids even as I aim for my 5th decade in ministry there seems to be more challenges for those of us in ministry today, like no other time in history. I believe this book is a game changer

for people in ministry no matter how long or how short you have been on your ministry journey. The wisdom Trisha gives and the research she presents is just pure gold. If you're serious about finishing strong and being faithful for the long haul then read this book!
Jim Wideman
Kidmin Pioneer, and Family Pastor at The Belonging Co. Nashville, TN
Jim@ThinkDifferent.coach

As a Church Leader in Children's Ministry, I know what it is like to have high blood pressure and other health/family issues as a result of stress from my local church. The stats and truth that Trisha shares in this book are staggering. There is a reason Jesus calls the church to unity of mind and purpose, and I think every person who claims to be a part of the global church (and who loves their church leaders, volunteer and paid!) should read this!

Anne Marie Gosnell- Author of Matteo's Choice, Founder of www.futureflyingsaucers.com.

With thanks and love to my husband Scott, our children Logan and Eliana, my parents and all of our family and friends who prayed, encouraged and read rough drafts. Thank you for putting up with all the late nights!

A special thank you to my professor at Bethel Seminary, Dr. Denise Kjesbo, who oversaw a lot of this research for my degree and to my classmates in cohort G!

Thank you also to my editor/encourager Rev. Joe Bridger- I think you and I both have LIVED too much of this book in our own lives! Thank you to our illustrator Gene Peelman from GenoStudios. We so appreciate your gifts and talent! www.behance.net/genostudios

Thank you to all the pastors and spouses who shared their stories for this book. Names and locations have been changed to protect anonymity.

This book is lovingly dedicated to all those men and women who serve the body of Christ in ministry, whether you are full time, part time, bi vocational or unpaid. These pages are submitted with a prayer that you will be in ministry for the long haul.

Introduction

On my first Sunday at a new children's pastorate, I walked down the hallway toward the children's auditorium, just as a teacher came charging out the side door with a child wrapped around her left leg. The child bit a hole in the teacher's pant leg and howled, "I hate you!" The teacher glared at me and growled, "I'm so glad you are finally here so I can quit!" I'll admit, at **that** moment, I had thoughts like "What did I just sign on for?" Thankfully a good pastor friend of mine, called me during that week to tell me, "Trish, don't give up yet. You have to be there awhile to effect any real change." He was definitely right. That day was the start of some of the best 7 years of my **life**! I'm really glad I stuck it out. But it took a few miracles, a lot of hard work and quite a bit of **time** to see that happen.

But just how important is **time** to success in ministry? According to a recent study by Lifeway Research, the average stay of a pastor is just 3.6 years[1]. We have all seen ministry leaders quit long before that. But in this study, it was those who STAYED in one place for several years that had a higher chance of growth and success. If the key to success in ministry involves staying power, why are too many leaders leaving so soon, perhaps right on the threshold of amazing breakthroughs? And how many congregations are living with hurt and distrust, due to one

---

[1] Rainer, T. (2014, June 18). "The Dangerous Third Year of Pastoral Tenure" Retrieved January 7, 2015.page numbers needed.

too many leaders leaving? Nobody likes being used as a stepping stone. There is a lot of damage done to the kingdom of God, the church and to the ministers themselves, by too much turnover. Have you ever wondered how that could happen? How someone could go into a new ministry position bursting with excitement, creative ideas and bright dreams, just to turn and walk away months later? It's not like you wake up one morning and suddenly exclaim, "Oh wait! I forgot I hate writing messages. I'll go be a plumber." There must be other factors at play here, and the most popular guess is that ministry doesn't pay enough. Well, if you came into ministry for the amazing salary, you definitely had the wrong guidance counselor. For various reasons (other than money), many ministry leaders will be sorely tempted to walk away this year (perhaps even you).

This is a time when, arguably, the church needs passionate leaders more than ever. The field is truly white for harvest! For my degree at Bethel Seminary, I set out to discover the top reasons why pastors leave ministry. I also wanted to discover what could be done, perhaps through better training in our colleges, and systemically through the way we "do church" in a modern age, to keep pastors in ministry. Here I am sharing what I found with YOU, dear reader. My heartfelt thanks must go to every minister who shared their painful story for this book. Of course, names and locations have been changed to protect anonymity. My desperate hope is to encourage pastors on the edge of quitting to get healthy, and stay in ministry. We need YOU!

If you also are interested in why so many pastors quit, please read on. Let's explore the top warning signs that you, or a key leader may be close to quitting, and then learn the strategies to help YOU go the distance.

Father, Father, help me stand
I fear that I have fallen and
The strength to one day rise again
Is hidden in your hand

Blinding heartache, pain inside
Fear that binds my mortal mind
Wounds too deep for a friend to find
Are open to your eyes

Who else has tasted of my fears
Cried my cries and wept my tears
Restored the empty wasted years
When the future was unclear

You visited this world below
You wept with us for human woe
Your foot has walked this narrow road
My way, Dear Lord, You know

Father, Father, help me stand
You're here where I have fallen and
Tomorrow I will rise again
Still holding to your hand

-Trisha Peach

Chapter 1- Ignoring the Warning Signs

With shaking hands, Ben fumbled for the door lock on his Toyota Prius. Unlocking the door, he wiped the sweat off of his forehead, took one last deep breath and got out of the vehicle. Best to get this over with, as quickly as possible. As he walked through these familiar halls on his way to the boss's office, images, feelings and memories from the last 2 years flashed through his mind. "I spent so many hours here every week...why does this building look so different now, so empty, so foreign?" Ben swallowed down a boulder of emotion, and with shaking hands knocked on his supervisor's door. Ben thought his heart was thudding so hard that everyone in this outer office area must be hearing it. "Come in" came the answer from within, and Ben entered the office, just as he had hundreds of times, only this time was different. Because this time, Ben was done. His boss did not look up, did not seem to sense what was about to happen- what had already happened many, many months ago. Ben's boss continued to text someone one handed, while she held one finger up asking him to wait. Without ceremony, Ben stepped forward and silently placed a letter on her desk. He felt like throwing up in her trash can. "How did the great plans for this position go so horribly wrong?" His boss absentmindedly picked up his letter and gave it a cursory scan. Ben watched the emotions in her face change from confusion, to disbelief, to shock, to ... "Ben, you can't be serious? You are resigning? Why? We certainly did not expect that. Let's sit down and talk about this. You had an amazing quarter just now. I do not understand. Can we talk about this?"

But what she did not know was it was too late, FAR too late, for any discussions or working towards solutions at this point. His eyes were cold. His supervisor was struggling to catch up- why was this happening? But Ben wasn't there to talk about his options or his frustrations. Ben was FINALLY making his supervisor aware that he had quit, given up on this position, in his heart...months ago. Everything in him had DIED for this place, and nothing would ever bring that back.

We've all heard the dramatic stories about the people who have a bad frustrating day, and then throw an epic tantrum, stomping off the job like a two year old, with a loud echoing cry of "I QUITTTTT!" But the reality is that most of the time, when a leader announces that they are leaving a position, it was not a snap decision for them. Their decision to quit was made over time, and made long, long before they chose to announce it.

Many supervisors say they did NOT see the resignation coming. So are there ANY signs at all that you or someone you work with or someone you supervise may be in danger of quitting/leaving their position? How can you know if your heart is leaving that position, even before you have acknowledged that feeling? Here are a few warning signs that someone is in danger of quitting a job-even one they once loved:

1.You just don't care anymore. You cannot shake apathy. Something doesn't go well, or you exceed your goals- and it doesn't faze you either way. Something inside you has died. Once the pastor begins to "go numb" from burnout, then "depersonalization" often sets in[2]. This means that the pastor stops being able to truly care for their congregation or themselves properly. This is a negative coping method characterized by withdrawing from conflict and difficult situations rather than facing them. Whether a service or a program went well or was a disaster, he or she no longer cares. **I encourage you to talk about those feelings with your senior leader** and someone you trust outside your organization. It could be you just need a break, or a sabbatical etc. But you cannot ignore that apathy for long- it is SAYING something.

2.You are almost ALWAYS frustrated, irritated and resentful. It's perfectly normal to be frustrated at times (especially Mondays!). But if these feelings or anger and hurt and resentment have gone on and on and nothing you are doing is helping; it may be time for you to leave before that attitude gets worse and/or poisons those around you.

---

[2] Lee, Cameron. *"Dispositional Resiliency and Adjustment in Protestant Pastors: A Pilot Study."* Pastoral Psychology59, no. 5 (2010): 631-40. doi:10.1007/s11089-010-0283-x.

3.Vision is gone. You are no longer hoping or planning for great things a long way off there. You can barely focus on planning for this coming week. Planning for a year from now is nearly impossible. Because you can no longer see the future for your area. Planning projects further out is becoming more difficult. Many leaders have told me that when it was time to leave, they "felt it lift"- their vision and desire for that place was gone....so much so that the building itself began to look different to them; nothing seemed the same.

4.You find yourself often daydreaming about a different position/ministry/church. A lot of leaders have that awesome daydream of filling in for Francis Chan for a Sunday, or having a magazine article written all about their exploits. But if ALL you do is hope and dream about something else, somewhere else, then your heart may have died for where you are. And that's not fair for the people at your current place of employment. You should still be able to dream for the church you are CURRENTLY at.

5.You are now there for the wrong reasons- ie. money, habit, fear. You do not want to be there at all, but you just don't know how to do anything else. Or you are afraid of going somewhere new. Which leads to a great question: Why are you staying?

_____This should not take a

whole lot of time to figure out. If this takes a great deal of thought, or you cannot come up with a reason to stay, there's a serious problem.

6.Your giftings do not "fit" with the church's new vision/direction. You're not being used to fullest potential; you're just not challenged anymore. It could be that God has grown you so much in that ministry, that He now has plans for you elsewhere. And it could just be that - and please please hear my heart when I say this- you may not be what that church is looking for in a new season. Everything changes, always. And your giftings and leadership could just be an answer to prayer and a perfect fit somewhere new. I remember, many years back, sitting around the table at our weekly staff meeting at my church. I had been on staff there for several years, with a lot of growth and success. But increasingly, I was finding myself frustrated at these meetings. With the new leadership, new vision and direction, I had been so excited, but week by week I felt like a fifth wheel. I prayed about it, sought wise counsel, talked to the new lead pastor, and worked harder to make it work. But one morning, sitting in that meeting, reigning in a volcano of frustration, I took a good look around and realized....I was what didn't fit in this picture. It wasn't the 6 other staff who needed a change- I wasn't right for this newly redefined position. And I knew it wasn't going back to what it was. In that moment the whole picture changed. I felt a relief wash over me, as well as sadness, grief....but when we got up to leave the room and go into the hallways, nothing was the same. I knew it was over. I did keep praying, thinking, grieving, but God confirmed through several other people that it was time to go. I listened and moved on to an amazing new staff position that has been one of the greatest experiences-and most challenging!-of my life. And I got to see the next kid's ministry grow exponentially, and I grew in team building by matching myself and others in their skill sets. I know that if I had been stubborn and stayed without God's blessing, my ministry there would NOT have kept growing, and I would have continued feeling stymied and frustrated. And furthermore, things like my Africa trip, traveling/speaking, and my books may never have happened.

Ministry takes a lot of wisdom and prayer. And remember that God is still guiding, still writing your story and the stories of the ministries where you work. "He Who has begun a good work in you, will be faithful to complete it." Believe that in time, He will make His will clear to you. Just be willing to jump in and follow it. And be patient, prayerful and act with integrity in that "waiting time". God bless your ministry now and in the years to come!

"I think it was one of the hardest days of my life. I had just resigned my position on staff at a large church, mainly because of unrelenting conflict that I just couldn't take anymore. My spouse called and asked me to pick up a pair of boots at a store on the other side of town. It was sleeting badly outside. Without thinking, I set out driving the way I always did. I had been to that store so many times. And that road went right by the church I had worked at. As I passed, I wondered briefly, "Why is the parking lot so packed on a Tuesday night?" The answer hit me like a sledgehammer to the stomach. It was Christmas Eve. It did not feel like Christmas Eve for me. And inside that church were people I loved, people that were more like family, celebrating the birth of Christ together- doing the candle lighting ceremony I had done a thousand times. Only this time, it was without me. The enormity of the loss came crashing down on me again. Despite the sleet and snow, I pulled over to the side of the road and wept. I felt very alone and "outside" of God's house. When you leave a ministry position, you lose it all- friends, support, income, place of worship, traditions- you name it. It was tough, but our family is back in ministry. Many great days were ahead of us. But that day, is still seared into my brain.

-A.J.

Chapter 2- Transition Fallout- WHEN IT ENDS

Maybe you saw it coming, or maybe it hit you out of nowhere like a Mack truck into a 711 convenience store at 90 miles an hour...The ministry you were living and breathing, has come to an end. It may have been abrupt- a new senior leader came in and several (or all) of the staff leaders are gone. Or the congregation voted, and out of nowhere, you are now just OUT.

The change could also have been a long time in coming; a ministry and/or minister on life support, just waiting for that new ministry position, feeling and sensing things coming to an end- and then at last- the finality of announcing that you are moving on.

Bottom line: This is a time of transition. And there is a ministry loss involved (the loss of one before a new one comes).

Whether or not you knew this was coming, we are rarely "prepared" for a ministry loss. We all hope to be at our church "forever," and yes, we've all heard the stories of "He was at that church for 47 years and died in the pulpit" but the reality is this: MINISTRY POSITIONS END. Most positions are not forever. Only a very small percentage of ministers get to stay in one place more than 5 years. Almost all of us will have to deal with one or two ministry transitions along the way. I want to encourage you and give you any small insight I can to go THROUGH a transition WELL. Transitions are tricky- and involve some level of pain. TRANSITIONS ARE ONE OF THE HIGHEST RISK PERIODS THAT A PASTOR MAY QUIT MINISTRY ALTOGETHER. As a staff pastor at a very large church, I saw countless staff come on board, leave for new ministries, or be let go, or have their positions eliminated. Some knew what was coming and others did not. I have also left positions and taken new ones a couple of times in my own ministry career- and I know firsthand how difficult that can be!

A good friend of mine unfortunately went through the horrible loss of an infant child, AND then a subsequent traumatic ministry transition. He pointed out the unexpected similarities between the grief of a death and the grief of a ministry loss. He pointed out that in BOTH cases, his ministry friends stayed away- perhaps not knowing what to say. In both cases, he and his wife felt isolated from the church family and their Christian friends- again, they probably did not know what to say. He states that potential churches were wary of hiring him after both tragedies, because they were not sure he was over his grief yet. One church even backed out of their agreement of taking him on as pastor after they found out he had recently lost a child. Both events took time to get over the grief, and perhaps even some wrestling with God. However, I believe the loss of his baby was a much greater loss, that has become a part of who he is. A ministry loss also seems to have a greater impact on our self-esteem and even our self worth than the loss of a person, especially when we find our identity in our "Job"- our ministry.

A ministry loss is still a loss and therefore needs to be grieved. So here are a few things I have learned (sometimes the hard way) during my own ministry changes and losses and from other pastors who have survived more than I ever will.

DO's and DON'TS Directly following a ministry loss/transition:

DO- give yourself some time to process the enormity of the loss. You have to allow yourself time to grieve. Many pastors have likened their exit from a church to a death- the death of something they loved very very much. Ministry is like NO other job on earth. You cannot understand if you haven't lived it. It's not just a JOB, it's your whole life. And the people of that church become your FAMILY, your support system, your counselors, your prayer partners. So when a minister leaves a church for whatever reason, they not only lose their source of income, their security- they also lose their place to attend church, their close friends, their support system, etc. They lose their entire way of life. And if you have a spouse and/or children, this adds another loss- watching them grieve as they say goodbye as well. It's also the loss of your hopes and dreams that you had for that ministry and that church-you are grieving the loss of the good that was, and the loss of a future that now will not be. Your whole heart and soul was tied up in those dreams. In a "normal" career, if you leave your job, your family will likely stay in the area, in your own home, with their current friends, in their usual school, with the support of their church family and friends. A pastor may lose it all when their church position is gone. Many times the church will bar pastors and staff from attending the church after they resign or are let go, to "assure loyalty to the new staff." The loss for the minister and their family can be all encompassing, involving a move to a new city, new church, new schools, new friends... Many pastors say they have had to go through all five stages of grief- shock, anger, sadness, bargaining and finally acceptance.

DON'T- rush yourself into a new ministry position too soon. Many pastors do this because they need the income. But you have to let yourself grieve. And don't stuff your feelings down; you're going to have to acknowledge them sooner or later. And it's not fair to carry that on to the next place of ministry and carry out your grief (or anger or mistrust) on that poor group of unsuspecting people. If you can remember back to when you were dating, you may remember cautioning someone, "Don't take the first person you see right after a breakup. Avoid the rebound person!" That advice holds true after a ministry "breakup" too. Your judgement may be clouded while you are grieving. You may not be hearing God clearly right now, and may inadvertently jump right from the frying pan into the fire. Which leads us to -

DO wait on God for clear direction as to your next steps. He hasn't forgotten you. He will tell you what to do. Say this with me:

God is the One Who called you so one person or one church cannot UNCALL you.

When God called you into ministry, He didn't turn to ask anyone's permission, and He doesn't need their permission to use you now. His gifts and calling are irrevocable. He still has a ministry for you- a future and a hope. Don't settle.

Don't believe the myth, "If I don't jump into a new ministry seamlessly, I'll never work in ministry again." That is simply not true. Remember that God opens the doors you are supposed to be in. Wait for His right door. Jumping right into any open church, too soon after a ministry loss, can result in depression for the minister, and frustration for the new church. It is important to move on to that new ministry because you are "called" to it, not because you are desperate and anxious to avoid dealing with the loss. Eventually you will have to deal with the grief of leaving a former ministry position. The new ministry position deserves your full attention!

DO find a great support system. You may have lost some of your best friends and supporters. You need safe people to talk to. You need to be able to rely on your extended family, friends and ministerial colleagues at this point. The key here is to find SAFE people to talk to who will give you wise, loving counsel and let you talk/grieve. Your network of minister friends and colleagues will be invaluable to you when you are ready to take a ministry position again. Several pastors have reported that their ministry friends seem to "disappear" during difficult transitions. It is important to find ministry friends, outside of your church, who will stand by you through all of the steps and changes in your ministry journey.

DO go for counseling if you can. There should never be any stigma on getting wise confidential help from a professional counselor. There are several articles detailing the benefits of pastors getting quality counseling. If a pastor is struggling with diabetes, I strongly suggest that they go to an endocrinologist and get well. If a pastor is dealing with a different ministry transition, or with leading in a "difficult" pastorate, I strongly suggest that they seek out a professional counselor. For more on how a counselor can be extremely beneficial to a pastor, check out these articles:

thinktheology.org/2013/10/24/five-reasons-pastors-should-seek-professional-counseling/

http://www.expastors.com/why-i-believe-pastors-should-go-to-counseling/

DO take a vacation. Take care of YOU. Get healthy. Work to improve yourself. DON'T just sit there. Go to a conference. Finish that book you've been planning to write. Go finish that degree. You cannot improve what happened; but you can improve YOU.

DON'T just talk to anyone who wants to talk to you about it. It's not okay to try to destroy the church, ministers and ministry at the church you are leaving- regardless of how it went down. And some people are NOT safe to talk to. They just want juicy gossip, and perhaps drama. They aren't going to help you heal, in the end- they'll just pour salt on the wounds. These are the kind of people who want to come tell you everything that is happening at the church you just left- who said what about you, what your replacement is doing wrong and how they took down your beloved jungle set in kid's church. You do not need those conversations when you are trying to grieve. I heard one pastor's wife tell her best friend, "I love you Amy. But if we are going to stay best friends, we cannot talk about everything going on at First Church right now. I need some time to heal. Our friendship has to be more than my former church."

DO forgive those who may have hurt you. The Bible says that we must forgive others as Christ forgave us (Ephesians 4:32). Not because they deserve it - because they probably don't. But for Jesus' sake. And for our own sake! We may not FEEL those feelings right away; but we make the DECISION to obey and forgive and the feelings follow later.

Above all, don't let a ministry transition take you out of your ministry calling permanently. Don't let a ministry loss come between you and your Savior. Know that Scripture tells us that God DOES vindicate in His time, not ours. Forgive and leave them to Him. You still have work to do.

Milo's Story:

I stepped through the side door of the parsonage and tossed my keys on the counter. I glanced at the clock. 6:30. Just another typical 11 hour beat down of a day at the office. The house was ominously quiet. My wife and 2 young children were back in her home state for a few days attending a funeral for her uncle. The senior pastor deemed it unnecessary for me to attend such an event because it was not MY immediate family, so I stayed behind. I ceremoniously opened the fridge. I had not eaten anything in almost 2 days, but I had no appetite. I plodded into the sunlit living room and flopped into my big chair, and reflected on my current situation. It was six months ago the first thought of resignation entered my mind. I quickly dismissed it because I had just moved my family across 3 states to take this position! I couldn't uproot them again. Not this soon. I would have to ride it out a while longer. Sure it will require effort, determination and prayer to do it, but it was perfectly reasonable because with God, all things are possible. I mean how much worse could it get? I had no clue.

My daily routine was not only to make sure I accomplished the laundry list the Senior Pastor's responsibilities that he delegated to me, but to also anticipate what tasks that were unmentioned that he may or may not also expect to be completed. Somewhere in between all of that, I could squeeze in an hour or two of taking care of the actual responsibilities that were pertaining to my position and area of ministry. It would either be a phone call around 8pm or a sit down meeting in his office the next morning where his laundry list would be examined and scrutinized to the minutest of details. The interrogation would not be concluded until an error was found. Whether it was an omitted task, or a phone call that was not made, or a thermostat that was improperly set, the size of the infraction was irrelevant. I would be berated and belittled as to my utter incompetence and general worthlessness. If on the off chance no deficiency with me could be found, it would be shifted to a deficiency with my wife, or my kids. How dare my wife mention a desire to get a part time job! "If she got a part time job the church might think I wasn't taking care of you!" I was instructed that I had better "get that woman under control"! I also needed to count my lucky stars I had HIM as my senior pastor because any other pastor worth his salt would have fired me by now. I wasn't the only lucky one on staff. The associate pastor looked just as gaunt and hollow as I did. We Divided our time at the whipping post evenly.

We had been there now 16 months, and things were bad. My situation was out of hand. My wife knew I was under a lot of stress and pressure, but I didn't tell my wife very much about the abuse I was suffering. It was because her positive and optimistic attitude was often the only thing keeping me on my feet. I knew that if I told her the gory details, her positive and encouraging attitude would go right out the window. I was too afraid to tell her the truth and cut that life line. Besides, it couldn't get any worse right? Oh it could get a lot worse. For the last 2 months I had begun to push back against these tirades. I was no longer just going to be ground into the dirt without at least attempting to stand up for myself. As a result, my "meetings" with the pastor became a lot more heated, frequent, and a lot longer in duration.

His wife was the church secretary, and unbeknown to me at the time, during these tirades she would call my wife, to pray with her that God would open my eyes to how much I was loved, appreciated and cared for by them. She would tell my wife that she needed to speak wisdom to me. She needed to help me understand that all intentions were good and benevolent. She needed to help me see the truth. That just about ended my marriage. Now when I came home defeated, exhausted and angry, my wife would begin to relentlessly interrogate me as to what went on at the office. As I would begin to unpack what happened and what was said, and HOW it was said, she began to defend the senior pastor! She would implore with me that I needed to understand that I was misinterpreting all of the verbal, mental and spiritual abuse. It was all for my benefit. Well, this ruse only lasted 3 weeks before her eyes were opened to the truth after she received an exceptionally viscous tongue lashing one day in our own kitchen. Even though the division lasted only 3 weeks it drove a massive wedge into our marriage. I no longer trusted my wife. I no longer respected my wife. I resented her deeply. After we fled the ministry, we barely spoke to each other for 6 months. It would be another 3 years before we could even have a minor disagreement about anything and not have me explode in a fury of pent up pain and baggage. It would be 5 years before I would stop holding it over her head and be able to let it go and start to forgive.

The tyrannical and duplicitous behavior of my senior pastor knew no bounds. His verbal abuse, mental and spiritual manipulations were unrelenting, without equal and without reprieve. Only the staff was aware of this fact. The senior pastor put on such a wonderful mask to everyone else that if I actually told the cleaning lady he referred to her as "the heifer with the sweeper" she would never believe me. I knew I had to resign. I had lost hope. I had lost all joy. I was losing my soul. I have to resign, but how could I do that to the Youth Group? The Youth Ministry was gaining serious momentum. We were seeing troubled teens turn their lives around. There was new spiritual life budding all through the Youth Ministry and the lives of the kids. How could I resign in the midst of that? The kids will be utterly confused and feel completely betrayed. If I resigned, it would all burn to the ground. How could I do that? I can't stay here, that much is obvious to me, but I can't leave either. There is no way out. Well... there is ONE way out...WAIT! NO! I snapped out of my fog of thought and reflection. I was sitting alone in the dark. It was now 10:30. What happened to the last 4 hours!?!?! Did I really just think about suicide?!?!? Okay, THAT'S not good! There is no way I am going to allow this man to steal my children's father from them! The next time he goes off on me, it's all over. Without fail, he did the next day, and I firmly resigned without hesitation or remorse. I had nowhere to go, but it didn't matter. I'd rather be penniless and homeless, but free rather than spend one more moment in this position.

The next 2 weeks would be the hardest of my entire life. Leading up to my resignation, the senior pastor and I had put on such a good mask to the church that nobody had any clue there was anything amiss in the office. He had to do damage control, and he needed to do it quickly. He told the board that I had suffered a "mental breakdown" and that they should not talk to me because of my "fragile condition". His wife told a few key gossips in the church that my wife was the reason I resigned because she threatened to divorce me. I had angry parishioners on my doorstep, one threatened to "beat me" for betraying the church and the pastor. (if only this person knew about all of the horrible things the pastor said about him) I also had a few people on my doorstep expressing sympathy because they suspected enough through observations... In 10 days we packed up our lives, loaded the moving truck, and I literally drove as fast as the truck could possibly go for the next 7 hours down the interstate.

I have seen the devil, and he pastored a church! I wrestled with how could a person like this become, and remain a pastor? The answer to me seemed fairly obvious. Nobody knows the truth about it! If nobody knows about it, that means the youth pastor hired to replace me will go through the same meat grinder that I just escaped. I would not wish that even my worst enemy. I had to let somebody know so there can be some accountability-ANYTHING to alter the current situation. I called my old mentor from college and asked for wisdom. He was aghast at what I was sharing with him. He told me he would be making some phone calls to his friends that held high positions within the denominational leadership. A week later he called me back to inform me that I would soon be receiving a phone call from the denominational director of the state I just fled. We prayed together briefly and he hung up. Five minutes later I received the call from the director. I shared the generalities of the circumstances surrounding my resignation. After only a few minutes he cut me off and said, "Look, your ex-pastor's church gives over $100,000 a year to the missions program. Do you really think a new pastor coming in behind him would keep up that level of giving? We both know the answer to that is no." I was stunned. I was dumbfounded. I was angry. I said with a shaking voice,

"Are you kidding me?"

"No I'm not..." And he hung up.

That was the moment. That was the precise moment when I vowed to never return to the ministry. I would never give my time, talents or my energy to anything as corrupt and dirty as the church ever again! That was the precise moment that I called God a liar and a feckless con artist. I yelled, I screamed, I sobbed until I had no more tears. For the next year I refused to pray, even over a meal. I was not going to give God the satisfaction. He abandoned me. He was a liar. Everyone's prayers fall on deaf ears so what's the point? I was in a dark, DARK hopeless place. My marriage was barely holding together. We went to church only because my wife insisted. I would physically twitch all through the service as memories would always flood over me. My wife was in a dark place as well, but she was not jaded and hopeless like I was. She still prayed. As a result of her prayers I came back around to God and Christ. I began to pray again. Through gritted teeth I began to forgive, and little by little I began to heal and let go. God began redeeming things in my life. God opened my eyes to how he WAS there with me through it all. God DID see what was going on, and He dealt with it. I found out later the senior pastor was caught in a felonious crime and was disgracefully removed from his office. It's 12 years later and I am in a good place now in every sense of the word. I am not in ministry, and I will never return to ministry. But my relationship with Christ, my wife and kids and myself are BACK."

Chapter 3- Unrealistic Expectations- Toss Those Rose Colored Glasses

"Oh just you wait," he said with a confident smile. "The last generation of pastors just did not get it. The early church 'added daily to their number', so that means that God has promised us at least 365 converts a year. I am claiming that promise; you'll see me pastoring a massive church within 5 years of leaving Bible college. And if the board gives me any static, I'll use my pastoral authority to tell them to hit the road."

This was an actual statement made by a Bible college student in one of my undergraduate classes. We had a joke back then, that if you want to know ANYTHING, just ask a freshman- they always know it all. I remember shaking my head in a mixture of pity and horror at this young man. Even though we were the same age, I grew up in the ministry, and I knew from experience that he had NO idea what he was getting himself into. More of my fellow graduates ended up quitting than stayed in the ministry. What happened to all that passion, zeal, ideas and dreams?

A key reason that pastors quit is that they go into ministry with some pretty unrealistic expectations.

Too many leaders leave seminary and enter the ministry with clearly unrealistic expectations. This "role dysphoria", which happens when talents and role expectations do not line up with the actual duties of the position, can quickly lead to frustration and burnout. Often the pastoral role is ill defined and varies by church, denomination and geographical location. Proverbs 19:2 is great for anyone contemplating a ministerial position, "Desire without knowledge is not good- how much more will hasty feet miss the way!"

Let's take a look at just a few of the most common *unrealistic* new ministry leader expectations...Did **YOU** go into ministry with any of these?

1.MYTH: I will only speak to adults (or children, or youth etc.)

REALITY: Gone are the days that this will work. In a day of family ministry, your communication skills with adults, parents, volunteers, children and staff will make or break your ministry there. You must be able to communicate well up front and in writing across generations.

2. MYTH: It's a church so there won't be any conflict. Everyone will love each other and pray all the time. I once interviewed a young lady for an administrative position in the children's ministries department at our church. I asked her why she wanted to work at our church. She responded, "I am fed up with the arguing and stress and politics of the business world. I would love to work at a place without that conflict,

without politics. I am looking for that peaceful slower pace!" I did not hire her. She loved attending our church so much, and I did not want to ruin that for her. And I could tell she just wasn't ready to handle the stress, conflict that comes with ministry. The stark truth is:

Ministry can be especially prone to conflict EXPLOSIONS, especially when that ministry involves people's kids, or a person's deeply held beliefs or the use of someone's personal giftings.

Unfortunately, handling conflict is part and parcel to working in the ministry (See Chapter 3 for an in depth look at the different conflict styles as well as suggested methods of dealing with ministry conflict.)

3. MYTH: Everyone (Christians) will love me, and see this vision that God gave me. My church will appreciate what I'm doing. They will jump on board to help once they see God moving and changing things!

REALITY: The truth is that many "religious" people did not accept Jesus' ministry, the ministry of the apostles or the ministry of the Old Testament prophets. You cannot please everyone or make everyone happy. So it is very important to stick with the calling God has given you. There will always be people who do not agree with the way you do ministry or the direction you are taking. The goal is to keep as many people with you as possible, yet to understand that not everyone will "make the turn." Some people will get mad and leave their area of ministry and/or the church as a whole. And that is ok. Keep pushing for the vision you know God gave you, get as many on board as possible, and release with a lot of love those who cannot accept the changes you represent.

4. MYTH: We will affect all of these changes right away.

REALITY: Nope. Andy Stanley said it best when he compared a church to a ship. He explained that the church is not a canoe. It does not turn "on a dime." Your church is more like the Queen Mary. And a ship that big does not turn on a dime. The older and larger your church is, the tougher it may be to effect real change. I remember being frustrated by the slow pace of change in one of my ministries. A good friend of mine kept reminding me, "Trisha, you cannot make all of these changes stick in a few months. It may take several years."This was encouraging to me, and I found that in general, he was right. This is scary considering the very short average stay of pastors at any one church....God's best blessings in ministry go not to the most talented, but to those who don't quit. This will take time. But the God Who called you will equip you. Be patient and keep pushing that vision for the long haul.

5. Myth: "If I do everything another leader/church did, I'll get those results right away. That will all work here too!"

REALITY: Some Most things will not change until you have put in a lot of work and time. <u>You may do what someone else did, and not get the same result</u>. It takes wisdom to know the timing of change and the priority of changes; too much too fast and your
team and families won't be with you. Sometimes the best thing to change first is the thing that is the least painful for the least amount of people.

6. MYTH: "If ministry gets too tough, I can always just do _____."

REALITY: Having "An Escape Plan" will harm the ministry you are trying to do right now. Burn those escape bridges and do what God has called you to do. **If you have a backup plan, you will use it.** If you build that emergency exit, you will use it. You are going to have to let go of your escape pod. Ministry can and will get that tough. Could your diet work if you said, "I'll just keep chips and ice cream stocked in the house, just in case this gets difficult?" That would be setting yourself up for failure! If you really want to eat healthy long term, you will have to get rid of your junk foods. The disciples didn't say, "Well, if this Jesus thing doesn't work out, we'll just go back to fishing." They were all in. And your church and your ministry desperately needs you to be all in. Determine in your heart to do what God has given you to do and stop planning an 'out'. Don't look back from the plow (Luke 9:62).

* keep my eyes on Jesus-never look away from him!.!

What are some of the misconceptions that YOU came into ministry with?

_____

_____

Did you know that many of the faulty expectations for a ministry position actually begin with the first interviews for that position? The time to take those rose colored glasses off is BEFORE you accept a position. You need to find out, as best as you are able to, what you are signing on for.

In 16 years as a full time children's pastor, I have done some interviewing in my time, and I have also interviewed many potential staff members. Along the way, I have compiled a list of some of the most important questions- essential questions- to ask very early on in the interview process. This list is of course not exhaustive, but I truly hope that anyone interviewing can find some of these topics helpful.

Here are a few questions you NEED to ask and have carefully answered BEFORE you accept a ministry position:

1. "Is this church looking for a Pastor or more of a Director/Administrator?" Before accepting the position you should

know if the job description is for a pastor, an administrator or a bit of both. Make sure to ask for a copy of the job description! When I look through pastor/director job descriptions I see many terms (buzz words) like "cutting edge" "relational" "team player" "family minister" "creative" "leader of leaders" "self starter who can hit the ground running" "not a one man (or woman) show". More and more churches, especially larger churches, are looking for more of an administrator to head up their programs instead of a pastor. The sheer volume of details involved with coordinating that many members requires more of a "Joseph" (or several of them) with a lot of wisdom and great organization. What is the difference really? Which one does your church really need or want to hire? Which one are YOU? Here's how to tell:

Pastor: Provides leadership, vision, strategy, recruitment, coordinates teams of volunteers and staff. They have a background/training in pastoral work/studies. The position or role is a pastoral role. As a pastor, this person baptizes, visits homes and hospitals etc- has a pastoral ministry calling.

Director: This person is more on the administrative side of things. Usually a previous pastor or pastoral leadership team have already provided the vision and direction for the church/department and the director is the "person in the trenches" carrying out that plan. The

Director typically does NOT have a background in pastoral ministry, but may be very gifted in organization, networking and communication.

Many positions are a mix of both of the above. <u>It is absolutely CRUCIAL that your understanding of your role is CRYSTAL clear BEFORE you sign on the dotted line and step into that ministry.</u> <u>Expectations MATTER.</u> If your church is expecting a "pastor" but you do not ever want to do baby dedications, baptisms, funerals, weddings etc- you may have an awkward clash of expectations. Or if, your church THOUGHT they wanted a visionary, strong leader and communicator/pastor, but what they REALLY wanted was a very organized administrator to carry on all of the programs that the former pastor had instituted, this is going to lead to problems.

2. Are you looking for someone to provide vision or to carry out a preexisting vision? If this position is a "director" position, managing a preexisting vision, who came up with the vision, and who is setting that vision now? (former pastor, senior leader, Family Life Director, a curriculum?).

3.Who chooses the curriculum we use? Am I locked into the current one? If so, for how long? Who would have to approve a curriculum/message series change?

4. What is an average schedule for a staff member? Do Sundays/Wednesdays count as "work hours" or will my 40+ be on top of that? What would be the designated day off (if they do not have a clear day off for you, this is a red flag). How many events are there per month? What is the expectation for staff at these events? How many evenings a week will I need to be at the church?

5. Does the church do evangelism/outreach? (not all do!!) What and how many outreaches and serving opportunities does the church do and how would I be involved?

6. What expectations would the church have for my spouse/children? Some churches expect spouses to attend all services/events as well. This poses a problem if your spouse has a career outside of the church. Am I required to attend any annual special prayer gatherings?

7. What are the expectations around holidays? Many churches expect all staff to be present for Easter, Christmas and other holidays. I've seen this come as a shock to many a new staff person who had to give up/redo their long held holiday traditions. There have been a few tears through the years when new staff members realize that we ALWAYS have Christmas Eve services every year and that NO ONE on staff is allowed to miss them. EVER. (If you allow one person to miss it, ALL of the staff will ask not to be there). These are "all hands on deck" services

for us- which means some sacrifices/rescheduling for the staff. Our holidays with our families are almost NEVER on the actual day of. Most of my family is in ministry so they totally understand. Other families who are not in ministry may have a tougher time with not celebrating on the day of. My husband's family had a tough adjustment, since they had a long standing Christmas Eve family tradition. It was unthinkable that any of the family would not be there. But reality set in that their son and I and their grandkids would never be able to be there, due to Christmas Eve ministry obligations. They ended up graciously flexing for a different day than Christmas Eve, but it was a painful few years of acceptance and transition.

8. What is the church's overall vision? If you are applying for a staff position, what is the senior leader's vision? This is crucial, because his/her vision for that area is automatically YOUR vision, which you must uphold and defend. If you accept that position, the senior leader's vision is what you will be working to bring to life! You have to be 100 percent on board with that vision. Is the overall vision and mission of the church something you can work within?

9. What is the church's official position on women in ministry? Is your denomination more "egalitarian"- meaning open to women in ministry and the equality of women and men? Or is your denomination more "complementarian"- meaning not open to women in ministry, believing

that women are a "complement", a supplement, to the ministry of men? Churches vary WIDELY in their official positions and their practices concerning women leaders. This is good to know whether you are a male or female applicant. A male worship pastor friend of mine was shocked when the church did not support his wife going for credentials.

10. How many staff members have they had (total in all areas) come in and go out over the past 3 years? If there was a huge turnover at one point, what was the reason? Too much staff turnover is usually a bad sign of leadership dysfunction.

11. What were the circumstances of the last leader's departure? May I speak with the former leader (I highly recommend it). Proverbs 18:17 tells us that, "A man seems right until his neighbor speaks." It is always a good idea to get both sides of the story. Perhaps you will still take the position, but it should be with your eyes WIDE open.

12. Who would I be directly reporting to? (I.e. If I have a problem, or a question, will I go to the senior leader or a family life director or elder??). What you are really asking is, who is your boss on a day to day basis? You may adore the lead pastor, but really have a rough experience reporting to and working with his wife/sister/uncle/etc.

13. May I see a copy of the church's doctrine statement? Many churches these days are "Community Church" or "Mountainville on the Rock" etc. which really does NOT tell you where the church stands on key doctrinal points- salvation, worship, baptism, miracles etc. etc. etc. A friend of mine accepted a position without looking into this, only to find out 3 weeks in, that the church (which was independent) did not believe in the Trinity. She ended up quitting shortly after. Even if you recognize the "brand" of the denomination, make sure you look at their doctrinal statement, and that you feel comfortable working under that. It is not fair to the church or to yourself to accept a staff position and then try to change the church's doctrine.

14. May I see a copy of the church's financial report? These are supposed to be available to anyone upon request. If the church is in financial trouble and/or is cutting back staff, better to know that up front.

15. I recommend "googling" the name of the church for research purposes. If the church has had recent public sex scandals or money scandals etc. you will want to be aware of that. (Some churches will NOT tell you about these.)

16. Will I be supervising staff? If so are these staff salaried or hourly? What are their job descriptions? Do I have hiring and firing ability over the staff I am supervising?

Give yourself a break: Even with the best of research, interviewing and preparing, each of us will encounter things in our area of ministry that we did not expect. And if you know that God has called you to minister in that certain church for this season, then you will only be happy and fulfilled if you are in the center of His will. But it is still best to have as clear a picture as possible of what you are stepping into. As Jesus Himself told us, "Count the cost" (Luke 14:28ff) (think about the full cost before you start). Lasting over the long haul in ministry is not so much about being obliviously naive, avoiding all risk or being constantly pessimistic. God never promised us things would be smooth or that people would like us. Jesus even warned us that we would be, at times, rejected. (John 15:20). God uses us most powerfully when we can realistically assess a situation, and then go in ANYWAY, sacrificing by faith, obeying Him with eyes wide open. And then God loves to surprise us by EXCEEDING those expectations with miraculous interventions. And no rose colored glasses needed.

"I'm sorry Pastor Trisha. My mom can't pick me up back here in the kid's ministry wing- she really can't. You see, she used to be a children's pastor, like you. And she was an amazing children's pastor. The kid's church was big and growing. She built a whole treehouse set- you should have seen it! Our whole family served in that ministry for years. I miss those days. It was busy but we loved it. Mom was happy. Now my mom usually drives way around to avoid seeing that place. But just last week, she suddenly pulled into that church's parking lot, put her head down on the steering wheel and cried and cried. I was so scared. I did not know what to do. I wish our family would be back in ministry together. I wish I could see her smile again. For a long time, we could not even go to church. Mom is just now able to start going to church again, here at this church. I'm so happy to get to go to church again! But she cannot go anywhere near the kid's wing. I love serving again in kid's ministry, especially because it brings back some of the best memories I have ever had. I really hope Mom will be a children's pastor again. Do you think she will?"

- Caleb, 15

Chapter 4- Life Support System Failure

Right this moment, off the top of your head, how would you answer this question for me? **"Who are the trusted people in my ministry and personal life who are 'holding up my arms', supporting me , encouraging me and holding me accountable?"**

If you had trouble answering this question, or if you had to really think about it to come up with an answer or your first thought was, "What's a personal life?"- you may need to build up your ministry support structure. Want to survive over the long haul in ministry? You need family, friends, great ministry connections, and a life outside the church. *No, that was not a joke*. No matter what an awesome rockstar leader you are, we are all still learning, and we need each other. Burnout itself is not the core issue; <u>burnout is just one byproduct of a lack of support structure</u>. Doing what you love should recharge you. If you are feeling burned out, it is likely because you are mainly doing what drains you, instead of relying on your team. Let go of that need to control, and instead spend your time investing in a team who will take on this great work with you. Yes, Jesus preached to crowds of thousands. But He spent most of His time pouring into His team of 3, then His team of 12 and finally His team of 70. Your MAIN job at your church position should be to raise up new leaders to take on the work of the ministry. **Your relationship with**

Jesus, your spouse, your family and your closest friends, should outlast your current ministry.

Long gone are the days of being a "Lone Ranger"- trying to do it all yourself, surviving and struggling because of your lack of delegation skills, and lack of accountability. Pulling human beings out of the kingdom of darkness into the kingdom of light takes the power of God, and a TEAM. **Your ministry will rise or fall on the strength of that TEAM!** Let's take a closer look at who needs to be on your "All Star Team," and what you need to do to make them stronger and healthier so you can also be stronger and healthier as their leader.

1.You and Jesus- It is all too easy to fall into the trap of confusing "working in a church" with "time spent with God." It is in the presence of Jesus, through prayer and the study of Scripture, times of worship, that we are "filled up" to minister[3]. An article in Christianity Today had this to say about their own study of pastors and prayer, "The amount of time spent in prayer and personal devotions raises questions about the vitality of many pastors' spiritual lives. While 52 percent report spending one to six hours in prayer each week, 5 percent say they spend no time at all in prayer. Furthermore, while 52 percent say they spend two to five hours a week in personal devotions unrelated to teaching

---

[3] https://www.baptistboard.com/threads/how-long-do-you-spend-in-prayer.5612/

preparation, 14 percent indicate they spend an hour or less in pe

devotions each week. We have to question just how effective their

ministry can be with numbers such as these."[4] It would be difficult to

build a relationship with ANYONE with only 12 minutes of interaction

per day! In our "Martha-like" busyness of our ministry schedules we are

missing out on the more important "Mary-like" sitting at Jesus' feet for

instructions. As ministers who work at a church, we may begin to

believe we "get a pass" out of meeting with God. This is so dangerous!

How is our passion and love for Jesus? Do we remember what it felt like

to be forgiven and freed? Do we remember our calling and why we do

what we do? Are we still doing all this for Him...or for some other

person/reason? Time with Jesus needs to become (or return) to first

priority in our lives- and keeping office hours is not a substitute for that!

Over and over again, studies have proven that spiritual resources were

the most important factor is surviving ministry over the long haul[5].

Pastors who maintained the regular religious disciplines of attending

worship services, prayer, and Bible study reported much lower levels of

depression and burnout than pastors who did not regularly engage in

spiritual practices[6]. This was the same for clergy spouses, however,

---

[4] https://www.christianitytoday.com/edstetzer/2009/december/how-protestant-pastors-pray

[5] Scott, Greg, and Rachel Lovell. "*The Rural Pastors Initiative: Addressing Isolation and Burnout in Rural Ministry*." Pastoral Psychology64, no. 1 (2014): 71-97. doi:10.1007/s11089-013-0591-z.

[6] Abernethy, Alexis D., Gillian D. Grannum, Carolyn L. Gordon, Rick Williamson, and Joseph M. Currier. "*The Pastors Empowerment Program: A Resilience Education Intervention to Prevent Clergy Burnout*." Spirituality in Clinical Practice3, no. 3 (2016): 175-86. doi:10.1037/scp0000109

pastor's spouses reported feeling like they had fewer spiritual resources that the clergy person had[7].

2.You, your spouse and your family- One of the worst casualties of clergy burnout is the Pastor's family. Pastors rank third for divorces among professionals. When asked why they are leaving the ministry, 1/3 of ministers cited "family reasons." This family stress is cyclical, in that ministerial stress exacerbates family stress, which in turn contributes to worsening loneliness and burnout. The pastor/spouse divorce rate is even higher when the couple is trying to minister through personal or community tragedy, such as natural disasters, criminal behavior, prolonged personal illness, or acts of violence. The bottom line is that ministry positions may come and go. When the smoke clears, your family is supposed to be intact. Therefore, your family is a higher priority than your current ministry, always. Outreaches and sermons do not magically happen. You have to intentionally plan, work and prepare for them. Our families need that same work (and more), planning and intentionality if they are going to survive and thrive.

3.You and Your "Outside" Friends- There are many aspects of the ministry at your church that are not safe, or appropriate, to discuss with non-staff members of your church. However, each minister desperately

[7] Fallon, Barry, Simon Rice, and Joan Wright Howie. "Factors That Precipitate and Mitigate Crises in Ministry." Pastoral Psychology62, no. 1 (2012): 27-40. doi:10.1007/s11089-012-0486-4

needs someone to talk to, and perhaps get advice from. The relentless pace of ministry also makes it difficult to maintain relationships outside the church body. It is essential to make time to nurture these "outside your current ministry" friendships. These "safe people" should be more mature spiritually and able to keep confidences. Overall, you need to know that you have a solid outside friend who will always be for YOU, giving you encouragement when you need it most and will tell you the truth in love- even when you do not want to hear it. These relationships are worth fighting for even through (especially in) ministry transitions.

4.You and Your HEALTHY Church Ministry Team: Is VERY important that your church staff lead out of the place of wholeness! But what exactly does a healthy ministry staff look like/function like? It is difficult to talk about a healthy ministry team until we define what an UNHEALTHY ministry team looks like, operates like. You may already be in a dysfunctional ministry team without realizing it. The people you minister with Sunday after Sunday and during the week are so crucial to that ministry's health and wellbeing. A healthy team can dream, work, pray together- seeing God do the impossible! Being in an unhealthy ministry team can be soul-crushing, disheartening- making you want to leave ministry altogether. You spend so much time with your ministry team; it is imperative that you do whatever you have to/whatever you can, to make sure that team is a healthy one.

I'll never forget the day before I left for Bible college. My dad, a Pastor for 24 years at the time, put his hands on my small 18 year old shoulders, looked into my eyes and said, "Kid, if you are going to survive in ministry, you need to remember- people are CARNAL. They are broken and sinful. ALL people. People in the church and outside the church. Jesus and His apostles loved those people enough to confront, forgive and lead them anyway, and so must you." I guess that's not your usual pre-college pep talk, but I am so grateful for his words, because they have proved true time and again in ministry. I have seen some dysfunctional ministry teams in my career and if you've been in ministry *more than a week,* so have you. During the years I have seen ministry teams' BAD behavior- and I've seen good solutions and BAD solutions. If you are in a broken system, you probably already know it. By definition a "dysfunctional team" is a team that is NOT functioning properly- it is not reaching its goals. A word of caution: if your team is left to itself, allowed to be dysfunctional for too long, the end result is an abusive, acidic environment that will repel quality, high capacity leaders. Great leaders will not stay for long. Kind hearted team members will get run over, chewed up and spit out. This should not be happening in our churches- and yet it so often does. So what are the main indicators that your team is operating in a dysfunctional manner?

Here are a few major red flags:

A. Too much turnover- Some staff and key volunteer turnover is normal and to be expected. But when that becomes too much, there is a problem. I can understand one or two "bad eggs"- or wrong person or wrong position. But when too many people are leaving, this is clearly a systemic problem that must be addressed. Steps must be taken to correct the underlying issues that are causing people to leave.

B. Too many excuses- When a problem is clearly identified, what is your team's FIRST response? Is it problem solving or excuses? Excuses do not fix the problem. And your ministry team is supposed to be working together to solve problems- not to come up with better excuses. Anyone can give excuses. A dysfunctional team goes on ignoring, placating, and even rewarding all the excuses instead of confronting complacency and rewarding those who get their work DONE. Are you participating in a system that rewards failure by keeping good people who are doing their jobs in bad ways?

C. Constant blame- Again, the focus must be on solving problems and achieving our goals TOGETHER. A dysfunctional team's main focus is "whose fault is this?" The team spends whole meetings on finger pointing and placing blame. Finding fault, however, still doesn't solve the problem or get the job done. In fact, constant blame makes your team reluctant to take on any new responsibilities, challenges, or risks.

And you MUST risk in order to grow. We must ask ourselves the question on a team level. Are we creating an atmosphere of fear, hiding, and putting on fronts? The focus MUST shift from "Who are we going to blame for this?" to "How will we solve this as a team?

D. Leadership will not take responsibility- It is always "someone else's fault." True leadership must make the tough decisions and "own" the results (good and bad) of those decisions. Otherwise, the team will not have trust or confidence. A team will only put up with blame, excuses and weak leadership for so long...then they will either shut down or leave. When the team or the leader makes a decision, then they need to stand by it in unity. A healthy team does make mistakes and admits those mistakes. A healthy team actively fosters an atmosphere of respect and trust. This team will accept risks and rise to challenges!

E. There is no accountability- An unhealthy team cannot ask questions about where the organization is headed, how money is spent or why decisions are being made. Usually a dysfunctional ministry team says, "If you ask about my motives or my decisions, then you don't trust me. Just trust me and let me do whatever I want to. Christians let Christians do whatever they want. That's grace." Actually, accountability is BIBLICAL. Do not trust any leader who refuses to be accountable, open and transparent. Accountability protects YOU and your ministry.

Nothing destroys a church/ministry like a money or sex scandal. Protect each other!

F. A toxic environment is ALLOWED- This is a ministry team that allows, and refuses to confront, very bad behavior in its members. Gossip, pouting, shouting, threats, silent treatment, sharing confidential information, lying, hurtful talk, put downs- all of these are NOT Christlike and should NEVER EVER be allowed on a ministry team. And yet they so often are. **If you go home in tears on a recurring basis , or you are losing sleep often- you are probably on a dysfunctional ministry team.** If you are the leader of a ministry team like this, it is your JOB to confront this bad behavior head on. You set the tone that your ministry team will be a safe place, to encourage each other, pray for one another, share ideas and solve problems. Ministry should not be a shooting range to humiliate anyone. If you do not put a stop to toxic activity in your group, you will lose great leaders who no longer feel safe. **"Grace" does not mean you allow a wolf to shred your sheep to pieces in the foyer.** And what if you are not the leader of the group? That does not mean you are powerless! This is the time to use your passion for that ministry and lead UP! Write out your thoughts in a concise manner, and book a meeting with that leader. Have an uninterrupted frank discussion with that leader. Tell them exactly what you want to see change, and ask for action. Too many leaders say, "Well

I had to leave because the leadership wouldn't do anything about the dysfunction." But they never actually met with the leadership about the issues; and that really isn't fair. Don't assume, if you haven't tried.

G. Only a fraction of the team is engaged- Sometimes only a "cool table" club of the team is engaged in idea sharing and decision making. The rest of the team is not included, or used to their full potential. This usually means that you, as the leader, will have to actively pursue the input of your introverted team members. You will probably need to ask them directly, "What are your thoughts on this?" Remember to wait patiently for an answer. Another strategy would be for you to ask ALL team members to send you an email of what they liked about the proposal, and what they are concerned about with the idea within the next 2 days. Some team members will say more in writing than they ever would in a face to face meeting. Bottom line: your whole team should be engaged and contributing. Are you developing each other, growing as a team? Or are you letting one or two louder ones dominate every meeting? Your quieter ones probably have amazing ideas too; and if they stay quiet they may feel useless, frustrated and it will begin to show in their ministries. Intentionally engage each member of your team; do not allow it to become an "us" and "them".

H. You do not pray together- The focus becomes blame, excuses and cool clubs- not doing spiritual warfare together. The best way to start correcting that is to start MAKING time to pray together, learn together, grow together, do service projects together, and have FUN together. Ephesians 6:12

Ministering to your TEAM should be one of your number 1 ministry goals this year. So how do you build a stronger, more unified team? The teams I have led, and been on over the years have become more of a family, and I am so blessed to be a part of them. Whether you're leading a team of volunteers, volunteer department heads, paid staff or all of the above, these ideas you'll see below have worked for me and other ministry leaders, to build a winning team (and this includes your family). Here are a few steps in the right direction.

A. Pray together- There is power in praying all together with one purpose. Pray FOR each other as well. It is a lot tougher to stay angry with someone, when your hand is on their shoulder in prayer for their upcoming surgery. This time spent in prayer together should not be "optional" or an afterthought. I cut 15 minutes of every outreach practice time just so we could spend that time in prayer together. It changed EVERYTHING- attitudes, effectiveness of "performances", and our focus on the unchurched people who attended. Praying as one team can bond us in a way that nothing else can. No one ever said, "Boy praying was such a waste of time." If someone does, you know your problem member in the group instantly. Everyone can appreciate a team that begins and ends all of their gatherings with prayer.

B. Grow together- Have you ever gone to a conference by yourself? You have this AMAZING experience, epiphanies that change your life! And then you come back to your church and try to explain those moments, those feelings to your team? It's almost impossible isn't it? The old saying is all too true, "You just had to be there." Everything changes when the team returns together from a training/conference with a more unified vision, and everyone at the table "gets the inside jokes" and has the same memories of the event. You do not have to get them all excited or try to explain the experience, because they went through it with you. Other ways to grow together would include doing a book study or a Bible study together- we have had a LOT of fun bonding over our book/Bible studies! You can also find inexpensive local trainings to attend as a group or hire a speaker to come in and do a training for your team. A great newer option would be to do a live streaming training or conference and watch it all together at your church (or a neighboring church).

C. Serve together- Nothing, and I do mean nothing, seems to bond a team like working long hours on a major project. When you have a community outreach, vbs, service project, musical, Easter or Christmas function, it is good to have "all hands on deck" and give every member of the team an assignment. This laser focus- everyone pulling together in the same direction- everyone going for the same win, can show the "real side" of the people you minister with, the good, bad and the ugly. We get to know each other for REAL, and still love and appreciate one another for all of our unique giftings. We experience firsthand the power of working as a group towards a common goal. This usually attracts new team members who want to be a part of something that is succeeding and rewarding (Great teams are the best recruiters).

D. Dream Together- Is your "team" still a hierarchy of "I say and you do and don't ask why?" A much better is the model is, "Let's do this together, and I'll help you until you can teach it yourself." I highly recommend Andy Stanley's approach to team leadership out of his work The Next Generation Leader. Also, Dave Ferguson's Exponential is another great book about planning together as a team.

When you sit down to plan your calendar of events for the next year (which I really hope you are doing), who is sitting around that table? By that I mean, who has input in the planning of events and the pitching of new ideas? This can be scary to some leaders, and it definitely takes a lot of trust. But great ideas often come from diverse teams, even quiet, introverted team members. Perhaps your team members have been doing a lot of thinking and just need the chance to let those ideas out. They'll think of great innovations and solutions that you never could on your own. It's about letting go some of that need to control for the greater good of the people you minister to. Make it a safe place to express ideas, and even constructive criticism. But never allow pouting, grudge holding, or gossip. You can reserve the right to the final say, and you can always shut down negative or argumentative talk. But allowing a few more people at that planning table will not only uncork amazing creative conversations, but when you actually DO begin to implement your new ideas, you will have your teams buy-in and eager support, BECAUSE they had some say. BUY-IN always comes from IN-PUT. :)

E. Play together- It's official; teams that play together, stay together. If the only time you contact your team is when you want something from them (work related), they may start to feel used; they may also dread it when they see you coming (just more work to do). Don't just see people for what they have to offer you and "your" ministry. These are people, with lives and joys and hopes and jobs and families. Go to their sports games and cheer them on. Go as a team and do something fun- bowling, roller blading, boat ride, mini golf, a concert etc. I also highly suggest that you eat together. Sharing meals together has been known as a bonding activity throughout history. Go out to eat together as a team after services. Better yet, go to each other's HOMES and COOK together. Being a team means caring about people's lives OUTSIDE of the job you are trying to do together. If their child is sick, pray together for that child. If one of your team is in the hospital, go visit them together. As they say at Willow Creek, you are not just doing a job together, you are "doing life together." You are building relationships to last for the long haul. These relationships give birth to the best, most successful ministries you will ever know. Last year I visited 242 Community Church in Michigan. Their church has a tag line they end every service with, "Let's go be the church where we live, work and play. They have grown to 6,300+ people in 14 years. This is a church that believes in the power of Christians doing ministry (and life) together.

What kind of team are you dreaming of? The best things in this life don't just "happen"; they are intentionally planned and crafted. Put the majority of your time into growing a unified, effective team this year, and you'll be surprised how far you'll GROW. Here is a sample calendar from a different church. I like how each event is color coded, which is what my church uses too. What to create your own calendar for YOUR staff? Many times you can find one on your computer already, in Word or Microsoft Office. Many free templates exist on line. Here is one free site:

https://www.freechurchforms.com/free_yearly_calendars.html

When the smoke clears what is most important needs to be intact. Ministry positions come and go but your relationship with Christ, your family and your true friends should go the distance. So let's commit from here on out to stop putting most of our time into doing things ourselves and start putting the vast majority of our time into building up our faith, our family and strong TEAMS. And then...buckling our seatbelts for exponential ministry and personal growth, not for 5 years but for a LIFETIME!

"My good friend Kyle barely looked up when he spoke. He kept staring at his egg McMuffin instead of eating it. 'I'm done Dan. I will never be in ministry again.' It had been only 4 weeks since I had seen him last. He looked like he had aged 15 years. His eyes were beyond defeated. I had known Kyle and his wife Janice since college and they were committed and caring pastors. During that time, they had struggled with infertility and finally, by God's grace, they had a baby boy. Just 2 weeks before little Stephen was born, the new overseer terminated them both and hired new people. It wasn't for anything they had done wrong. Since they had lived in the parsonage, they were now pretty much homeless. A friend of theirs had taken them in while they searched for a place to live. According to Janice, there was little joy in their son's birth. She said that the whole time she was in labor, Kyle sat next to her, head in his hands, weeping. I fumbled, trying to say something that might ease their pain, "You guys are so effective in ministry! I know someday when this is all behind you, that God still has an amazing plan for your life." Kyle's head snapped up. His eyes were now full of fire. Through clenched teeth he hissed at me, "Not a chance. That man told me this was God's will. He told me I would quickly find a place to be happy in ministry elsewhere. He's wrong. I want everyone in the world to see that our lives have been destroyed." I mumbled something like, "I love you guys and God does too. You will get through this. Your baby is beautiful..." It was just so so sad! I just don't know. Who won in this whole mess of pain? Not Kyle and Janice. Not the cause of Christ. I wish this story had a happy ending. But last I heard, Kyle and Janice did not return to pastoring and that whole topic of that time in their lives is still strictly off limits.

The worst part is, I saw myself in Kyle's eyes. I knew that I could so easily be out of ministry, soaking in my hurt and anger for years to come, from all the junk that has happened to me (not nearly as bad as Kyle's story). I feel like the enemy has taken too much already- taken out too many of us. He (Satan) shouldn't get any more of our lives, our ministries, our families or our happiness." -Dan B.

Chapter 6- Conflict Casualties

As far as I know, no one wakes up one morning and says, "Oh wait, I forgot I HATE ministering to people. I'll go be a plumber." And yet, as you may have already found out, there is a very high turnover rate in both paid and volunteer ministers. And why? Not enough budget? Too many families to handle? I don't think so. *The number ONE reason that you will be tempted to quit in your ministry, is the fallout from poorly handled church conflict.* The church should be a safe place that does not tolerate grudges, pouting, gossip, hate, disunity and the like. But all too often, these bad behaviors are still happening among Christians, even in ministry.

For those of you who chose to serve in the children's area, hoping that you could avoid a lot of the politics and arguing that can go on in a church- I am sorry to tell you that you were sadly mistaken. The cold hard truth is: There is no area in the church as prone to **explosive** conflicts as the children's area.

Are you shaking your head right now? Are you thinking "No way! We wouldn't have arguments or hurt feelings happening in our kid's area!" There are a lot of emotions involved when you are dealing with people's KIDS. Families may overlook a problem in the parking lot, or even put up with a service element they did not enjoy. But if their child gets hurt, or comes home crying, exaggerates, embellishes or outright lies- then the parents or guardians will want answers....from YOU. Have you seen the news specials lately about parents bullying teachers? Negative culture toward authorities often spills over into the church. And of course, we are ministering to people who need Jesus, as we all do.

Unfortunately, we cannot eliminate conflicts in the church. But if our ministries are going to survive, and thrive, we are going to have to get better at reducing and managing the disagreements that WILL occur. Truthfully many people in our congregations have no idea how to disagree in a Biblical manner. As leaders, we have to intentionally TRAIN and model to our people how God expects us to treat each other. Matthew 18:15 "If your brother sins against you, go and tell him his fault, between you and him alone. If he listens to you, you have gained your brother.16 But if he does not listen, take one or two others along with you, that every charge may be established by the evidence of two or three witnesses. 17 If he refuses to listen to them, tell it to the church."

With that in mind as our end goal, here are a few very practical ways to thrive through the conflicts that come your way. I really wish I had known some of these when I first went into ministry:

1."Do not make their emergency, YOUR emergency." How do you feel when you get and email, text, or phone call from a Senior Pastor, volunteer or fellow staff member wanting to meet with you and calling it an emergency? Here is the best, most eye-opening advice that my boss ever gave me. "Just because someone calls you, emails you saying something is an emergency, does not mean it is an emergency." That is giving that person too much power. Their "emergency" may take you away from important family time, much needed sleep, productive appointments and other ministry. Just because someone DEMANDS a late night meeting, or to see you immediately, does not mean you are obligated to do so. In fact, I routinely will wait a day or two, so they (and maybe me) have time to calm down and prepare. Boundaries are so important for your family, and for your health, and for relationship with Jesus Christ.

When someone calls you during family time, prayer time or personal time, let it go to voicemail. Then listen to the voicemail, but do not respond emotionally, or immediately. Think first. Is this a real emergency? Can I encourage they schedule an appointment tomorrow or later this week? If their relative has just been in a car wreck, by all means go. If they are sobbing because their daughter did not get the solo in the Easter service, that can wait until tomorrow (Yes, I have dealt this this one many times). You are not responsible to meet everyone's emotional needs. They have to deal with their own feelings. You can care, you can help- without being controlled. And if you set a precedent of always jumping and running whenever someone starts drama, you will always be jumping and running for every situation, eventually damaging your ministry, your health and your family. When we jump and run every single time someone is offended we are FEEDING that culture of offense- and FEEDING someone's need to CONTROL others, both of which run directly contrary to what Scripture teaches. There are people in our churches who are addicted to drama; these people need love, hope and healing. They do NOT need you to enable their addiction. People demanded that Jesus do signs to prove His ministry, miracles and bread from heaven always, but He told them "No." John 6:22-35. Matt. 12:39, Luke 8.

Nehemiah's critics demanded to meet with him because they were offended with him, "(They)said, 'Come and let us meet together...'" But they intended to do me harm. [3] So I sent messengers to them, saying, "I am doing a great work and I cannot come down. Why should the work stop while I leave it to come down to you?" [4] They sent to me four times in this way, and I answered them in the same manner." Nehemiah 3:2-4. You have to stay focused on the "great work" that God has assigned you to do.

2.On the other hand, do not avoid necessary confrontations. The Bible tells us to "speak the truth to each other in love." Ephesians 4:15 I was born and raised in the Midwest, where "Minnesota nice" is a real thing. One of my biggest regrets in my early ministry is that I let too many things "fester", becoming a bigger and bigger problem because I did not want to face the person. I hoped the problem would just go away. I tried to work around the problem/person. And most of the time, the situation became so much worse than if I had lovingly confronted this person and been honest early on. Remember: **_Conflict ignored is only conflict postponed._**

3.Social media and electronic email fails: Never ever ever ever EVER (times 2,135) work on a conflict or tough situation over email, social media, text or voicemail. I don't care what the excuse is. Trying to solve conflicts like that never leads to anything good. And it's not Biblical. We are supposed to GO to them and meet one on one with the goal being reconciliation. Email is notoriously misconstrued; you cannot hear someone's tone or inflection or their heart. Don't leave room for misinterpretation. As tough as it sounds, bite the bullet and meet with them one on one to sincerely work it through. DO NOT engage in conflict in any way other than face to face. If someone expresses anger etc. over social media or voicemail, do NOT respond in kind. Always, set up a face to face appointment (at the church or neutral ground is best).

4.Don't ever put anything in writing or voicemail that you don't want EVERYONE to read or hear. A good pastor friend of mine received an angry outrageous phone call from a congregant. Without thinking, he called back and left a curt message on her voicemail. She responded by tearfully playing his voicemail message over and over in the church parking lot the next Sunday morning to anyone who would listen. He learned a painful lesson that day. If you aren't comfortable with anyone and everyone reading what you wrote or hearing what you said, then don't say it.

5.If your one on one meeting does not go well and there is no resolution, you are not "off the hook" to attack that person, or gossip, or "get people on your side" even if that is what they are doing. Yes, Christians "should know better" but many of them do not. We as leaders are called to lead by example. The next step in Matthew 18 is meeting with them with one witness. This should be your supervisor, key deacon or Lead Pastor. And by the way, senior leaders always HATE being surprised. If you have a tough situation, discreetly talk to your leader or to your elder board or deacon board as soon as possible. Better they hear it from you first! It is not gossip to keep leadership in the loop, since your goal is reconciliation. Most importantly you know you are not facing conflict alone.

6.Do not delete emails or voicemails pertaining to the conflict- they may come in handy later with your supervisor or with the board. Realize you are dealing with an antagonist. And information is power in their viewpoint. Since they will not forgive, they will not delete or remove emails or other "evidence" of your "wrongdoing." For professional purposes, you should hold on to anything you have in writing that relates to the conflict for at least a year afterward.

7.As much as humanly possible- don't respond to angry letters, emails or phone calls at ALL, when you are sick, overtired, grieving a loss etc. Remember, you are NOT obligated to answer immediately. You sometimes have no other choice but to minister reconciliation when you are not at your best, but if you have ANY choice in the matter, delay the confrontation until you are at your best. This has been a big one for me to learn!

8.Cannot think of what to say in that moment? Clam up. "Silence cannot be misquoted."- African Proverb. Silence is one of your BEST defenses- don't say something that can be used against you. They will keep talking themselves into a hole. It's ok, and wise, to say, "Hm, I'm gonna take some time to think and pray about that, and I'll get back to you." Do not get pressured into making a final decision or a declarative statement because it's being demanded. For more information on this, check out

Antagonists in the Church by Kenneth C. Haugk Available on Kindle.

9.Do not respond to or acknowledge any anonymous emails or letters in ANY way. That's not Biblical. And it encourages wrong behavior. Teach people right off the bat, that wrong behavior won't get them anywhere. TEACH and model Biblical behavior. You TEACH people how to treat you.

10.Do not let the hurt and pain that people have attempted to inflict upon you keep you from your calling. As we discovered earlier, God did not need anyone's permission to call you. A human being did not call you and a human being cannot UNCALL you. But too many wounded ministers take THEMSELVES out of ministry, because they will not forgive and move forward. This is a tragedy. Scripture tells us that if we will not forgive others that God will not forgive us. And we all need a lot of forgiveness! There is no limit to the forgiving blood of Christ. But the lies we believe can be one of the enemies strongest weapons to take out ministers- unresolved anger and hurt that we believe we have a right to own in our souls will destroy us.

According to K.W Thomas and R.H. Kilmann, the expert developers of best selling conflict management instrument since 1974, we all have one of 5 distinct conflict styles that we naturally gravitate towards. However, different situations tend to call for different conflict approaches. Do any of these sound like the way you ordinarily react to conflict? These are the 5 styles as related by conflict management author J.D. Meier:

"Accommodating – This is when you cooperate to a high-degree, and it may be at your own expense, and actually work against your own goals, objectives, and desired outcomes. This approach is effective when the other party is the expert or has a better solution. It can also be effective for preserving future relations with the other party.

Avoiding – This is when you simply avoid the issue. You aren't helping the other party reach their goals, and you aren't assertively pursuing your own. This works when the issue is trivial or when you have no chance of winning.   It can also be effective when the issue would be very costly. It's also very effective when the atmosphere is emotionally charged and you need to create some space. Sometimes issues will resolve themselves, but "hope is not a strategy", and, in general, avoiding is not a good long term strategy.

Collaborating – This is where you partner or pair up with the other party to achieve both of your goals. This is how you break free of the "win-lose" paradigm and seek the "win-win." This can be effective for complex scenarios where you need to find a novel solution. This can also mean re-framing the challenge to create a bigger space and room for everybody's ideas. The downside is that it requires a high-degree of trust and reaching a consensus can require a lot of time and effort to get everybody on board and to synthesize all the ideas.

Competing – This is the "win-lose" approach. You act in a very assertive way to achieve your goals, without seeking to cooperate with the other party, and it may be at the expense of the other party. This approach may be appropriate for emergencies when time is of the essence, or when you need quick, decisive action, and people are aware of and support the approach.

Compromising – This is the "lose-lose" scenario where neither party really achieves what they want. This requires a moderate level of assertiveness and cooperation. It may be appropriate for scenarios where you need a temporary solution, or where both sides have equally important goals. The trap is to fall into compromising as an easy way out, when collaborating would produce a better solution."

What would you say is your most natural style?

_____

Which style do you find yourself using more often in church conflict?

_____

A few final thoughts:

1.If lead pastors, staff, or key leaders have been leaving a church in large numbers in a short amount of time it is red flag (high turnover). The leadership of the church needs to get to the bottom of why it is happening and work a positive plan to get the church on a track toward health.

2.Members of your church, staff, volunteers, or fellow pastors being deeply wounded in church conflict is never just "ok" and "business as usual." God is never ok with people being broken and spit out. Growing, healthy churches learn to address conflict and even learn to handle disagreements Biblically. No church is perfect, but the fastest growing churches have this in common: They are always trying to improve- and they do not use people as "disposable commodities."

3.Growing healthy churches do not gossip and complain about their leaders. But they do address problems and consistently address, problem solve and work toward resolution in an ever-changing environment.

Don't ever get in a situation where you are covering up flaws, refusing to discuss the issues, sweeping the injured people under the rug- that WILL come back to bite you. The church does have to use some business practices to manage money well etc- but it is still a church. God

...ssioned us to minister to people not manage money or buildings. People over programs every time. Integrity first!

Many Pastors have said that looking back, they have wished that they had asked someone to leave the church. By that, I mean, someone who, after countless attempts at discipline, correction, is still unwilling to listen or change. This person is actually your "tumor". They are hurting people- hurting your church. Perhaps you may need to speak the truth in love, address this painful issue before it hurts anything else and ask this person to go.

Conflict in ministry is something we all face. It's something Jesus and all the apostles had to deal with. You may not have done anything wrong; often your ministry will be doing the RIGHT thing and that is what causes the conflict to surface. This is simply because the devil is real and we live in a sinful world. . Don't give up! Keep focused on doing the ministry God gave you, and God will go with you through it with you.

Isaiah 43:2

Open Letter to a Former Friend

16 "I have told you all of this so that you will not go down the wrong path. ² You

will be thrown out of the synagogue (church). In fact, a time is coming when

those who kill you will think they are doing God a favor. ³ They will do things

like that because they do not know the Father or me.⁴ "Why have I told you

this? So that when the time comes, you will remember that I warned you."

Dear Friend,

I know it's been awhile. Quite awhile. But I thought of you today. I try not to

think of you, so that I can go on with life, but memories of you slipped in. I

wonder if you ever think of me. Would it surprise you if I said, that I really wish

we could sit down over coffee and talk? I couldn't have said that until lately- I'm

human, and I needed time. Somehow I do not think we will get that chance in

this life to have closure, to talk frankly. My attempts at the time were not

received. But if we had the chance to talk, there are a few things I would want

you to know. I really cared about you. I think that is what made everything so

difficult. If I hadn't cared so much, and respected you so much, I could have

gone along my merry way without a thought. But one of my personal flaws is

that I am a bit naive, and loyal to a fault. I thought the world of you and never

imagined you felt any different. When I found out the things you had done, it

wrecked me- each lie, gossip or manipulation felt like a separate knife wound.

And I felt REALLY behind, like the only one who didn't know. I was doing well

and determined for the long haul, until I found out that YOU were the one

trying to hurt me. Then all the wind went out of me, and a part of me just gave up. I didn't want to keep fighting, I didn't want to WIN anymore, because there wasn't anything left to win. As Jesus and David put it in Psalm 55,

> "*¹² If an enemy were insulting me,*
>
> *I could endure it;*
>
> *if a foe were rising against me,*
>
> *I could hide.*
>
> *¹³ But it is you, a man like myself,*
>
> *my companion, my close friend,*
>
> *¹⁴ with whom I once enjoyed sweet fellowship*
>
> *at the house of God,*
>
> *as we walked about*
>
> *among the worshipers."*

B. I was lying in bed one night, agonizing to God about you doing what you did and then going away....and I realized...**we are never more like Jesus than when we are betrayed, or mistreated and love anyway**. And He DID warn us, many many times in Scripture that these things WOULD happen to us. "A servant is not above his master...." And the enemy loves to cause division and heartache like this in order to damage ministers and damage churches and destroy good people. And most of the time the enemy is efficient and successful at what he does. **We are never more like the devil than when we lie, tear others apart, scheme, push for power and try to divide.** I don't want to become more like the enemy. I want to continue this journey about being more and more like Jesus. Ministers don't quit ministry because they get sick of preaching. They quit because of junk like this- because their heart broke one too many times.

C. Forgiving you does not mean agreeing that anything you did wa right or ok. You will never know the hurt or loss you caused. I do not think you will understand the tears, the nightmares, the sleepless nights....the difficult time trusting new friends. Forgiveness does not mean declaring that everyone someone did is ok. Forgiveness is saying "I'm leaving this with God, and you don't owe me anything anymore." I think of totally forgiving someone as finally being able to sit and have coffee with them (without throwing the coffee) lol.

D. I do choose to forgive you. Completely. I'm not perfect either. And without the grace and never ending love of God, I'd have no hope. I know that if I won't forgive you, He cannot forgive me, and I am DAILY in need of His grace. And probably sometime soon, I'll need someone to forgive me too.

E. I have not let this end God's work in my life. When God called me into ministry at the age of 8, He did not turn around and ask your permission. And His gifts and calling are irrevocable. He who has begun a good work in me -and you- will be faithful to complete it. As Joseph said,

[20] As for you, you meant evil against me, but God meant it for good, to bring it about that many people should be kept alive, as they are today. (Gen 50:20)

God is the One in charge of my life (and yours). I believe now more than ever, that he doesn't allow what He cannot redeem. God has used every chapter of my life, the good and the bad, and the not yet known to further His story. These past several years have been amazing- a new book out that is doing well, ministry growth, and a lot of travel. On my kid's missions trip to Africa, I had climbed a mountain with our translator on our way to home visits. I was so overwhelmed by the beauty all around me, and the realization of all God was doing there on a daily basis. And then....I realized that if it hadn't been for you, *none of this would be happening. I would have stayed right where I was, on a different path, "safe". God had used the hurt, the loss to fuel a much more important cause- HIS. And I laughed. Then I shouted your name from the top of that mountain "Thank you!!" I think the translator thought I lost my mind. :) God used you in a big way, and for that, I am grateful.*

I am so happy to hear that God is using you in ministry- and I pray that God continues to use you for His purposes and His glory. Because it's about Him and His work here on earth. And we cannot let personal "junk" get in the way of that. I pray you go and do great things for God.

And finally- Although I never wanted you to miss out on heaven, I definitely wanted you to have your own "solitary confinement" section of heaven so I never had to look at you again. I am sorry that I felt that way at one point. But now I know we'll be sitting together at His table someday very soon, both saved by grace. And I will love you then too.

And I'll even pass you the salt.

love always,

Trisha

Chapter 7- Landmine Explosions- Sex, Drugs and Money

Sounds like a movie trailer doesn't it? But this is not the latest Hollywood blockbuster. The reality of any church scandal can play out more like a heart-stopping horror show. We already talked about the number one cause of pastor/minister dropout- poorly handled church conflict. (see Chapter 4) Many testimonies exist that the, the politics of church are one of the primary causes of people leaving the ministry. However, NOTHING, and I mean NOTHING can stop a ministry, and eject you violently FROM a ministry FASTER than a SCANDAL. This is the shrapnel that rips through a churches, communities and hearts. If unchecked, it is a real threat to the very fabric of the faith communities we love and serve.

I've personally seen churches survive their building burning down, tornados decimating their town or a violent tragedy touching their lives. These times of stress and grief can cause the Body of Christ to pull together in unexpected ways. But churches have a FAR tougher time soldering on when it's their pastor, staff pastor or board member, who was caught in a scandal, when their trust has been broken- and the sordid details are all over the news.

For me, the pastor or church that believes, "A scandal will never happen to me (us). It cannot happen here." is at highest risk for stepping on a landmine.

The top 3 landmines that can do untold damage in your church are:

 1. A sex scandal (of any kind, but one involving a child is a nuclear bomb).

2. An addiction scandal (usually when one of the leadership team is addicted to a controlled substance or an externally damaging behavior like gambling, pornography or physical abuse).

3. A money scandal (embezzlement, fraud, misappropriation of funds etc.).

A dishonorable mention here would be when a pastor/leader is arrested for a crime other than those above- though that is a lot more rare. For this chapter, we are going to focus on the "Big Three".

Please note: The most important consideration here is NOT your church's reputation. The most important thing is protecting people(especially children) from being abused. Scripture tells us to avoid even the very appearance of evil. (1 Thess. 5:22). Sometimes no misconduct really took place. Perhaps no real mishandling of money occurred. But just the ACCUSATION can, at times be enough when you are not prepared to defend against it. Ever been to a magic show? Why are they so popular? Because our gut instinct is to believe perception is reality at initial glance.

The good news is that there are simple precautions you and your church can take right now, to better protect yourself, your church leaders, your volunteers and your parishioners from major abuses and accusations. Let's take a look at our top 3 "landmines."

Landmine #1- A Sex Scandal

"But please Pastor Trish, just this once?" her enormous blue eyes pleaded with me, "This is really serious. I need to tell you something. I need you to pray with me. Can we go to your office real quick. Please? I just need you to listen." With her white blond hair in pigtails, and tears welling up in her eyes, she seemed so very fragile and willowy. Her slumped shoulders were so very thin and she shuffled her tiny feet in her little dress shoes with glitter covered bows! For just a moment I forgot everything else in the world. I took her minute hand and took just two steps toward the door out of the room. But suddenly I came to my senses and remembered the training I had received in Bible college. The

same training I had just DRILLED into my AWANA leaders the past
Wednesday night. THE RULE that was posted IN our volunteer
breakroom.

THE RULE OF THREE.

"No less than three people can be in a room at any time for ANY reason. NO EXCEPTIONS."

Since I had just taught on this to my leaders, and we were all here in the large group room together, I wanted to set a good example so I decided to follow the rule. I turned to her and said, "Oh honey, we can pray in here. Just tell me right here how I can pray." She continued to pull on my hand and plead, "NO, not with all these people around. This is secret." UH Oh. I didn't know why, but now my warning bells were going off. Again I said, "Let's go into a corner of this big room and pray." This time she got angry, "Don't you care about me? Let's just go to your office!" I cautiously replied, "What if we go to my office with the youth pastor? The three of us could pray together?" Now her anger really showed. "No, it has to be just you and me." The hair began to stand up on the back of my neck. I took her hand and prayed with her right there, and then went on with my night.

The very next day, this girl accused her school teacher of sexually molesting her. In court, the charges were dropped. But it didn't matter. The teacher had already been fired and could no longer find a job in teaching. What I did NOT know, was that this was the SIXTH time this same girl had falsely accused a teacher of molesting her. The police later said that no matter what, they had to take each and every accusation seriously. The child explained in court that this was how she got her mother and her (absent) father to pay attention to her.

I know in my heart that if I had continued taking steps towards my office that night it would have been me. Do you think a false sex allegation cannot happen to you? Do you think a false allegation cannot happen to a woman? Think again. God protected me, by following the rule of three. And this rule has been breaks down into many different facets in our ministries. For example, if a leader does not show up and there is only one child in the room, then that class must be combined or another solution found because one leader plus one student equals 2. And that is not acceptable. EVER. WHY? Well, to be blunt, churches are often soft targets for pedophiles. It is inexcusable to not do EVERYTHING in your power to protect the precious children you minister to weekly. Step one is always -NO ONE is alone with a child. EVER. Anyone insisting on being alone with a child needs to be dismissed from your ministry as soon as possible. Why would they NEED to go off alone with a child? They don't.

So how can we do BETTER at implementing the rule of three and making our areas safer? Here are some great ideas that some churches are using to not put adults alone with a child:

A. Glass windows on all classrooms. Doors can be fitted with glass windows. This is the cheapest and easiest way to make this happen.

B. Open concept classrooms- meaning that all rooms are visible to each other, and only partitioned off by dividers. (The big problem here can be noise, of course).

C. Two teachers per classroom, or you close the classroom (we used to do this until we went to open concept all in one large auditorium).

D. Combine classes or rearrange as needed, but NEVER allow less than three to a room. Not even once.

Keep in mind that this rule is wonderful to practice not just for protecting the children, yourself and your volunteer staff- you can use it in your day to day church interactions as well. I will NOT meet alone with someone of the opposite sex; I will always have someone else there or the door open. I will not ride alone in a vehicle with someone of the opposite sex (this was also our church policy). I will not have a confrontational discussion with a parent or volunteer alone without a witness or at least an open door during office hours.

Lovingly confront and hold each other accountable. Do what you can to encourage healthy marriages among your staff and volunteers. If you hear of sexual misconduct, you MUST not sweep it under the rug. If a child is involved, you MUST immediately notify the police; Pastors and church leaders are mandatory reporters. If you suspect abuse or someone informs you about abuse, you tell your supervisor immediately and report it. You are not responsible to investigate the validity of any claims. **You ARE responsible before God and in a court of law to speak up for that child**. If you hear about two adults in your church that are involved in sexual misconduct (such as having an affair), this is not a criminal matter, but it certainly is a moral issue for the church-especially if these adults are in any form of leadership.

My mind immediately goes to a recent church scandal. It became public knowledge that 2 people on a worship team were having an affair (they were both married to other people). What made this so much worse was that the Small Groups Pastor had reported to the Lead Pastor months beforehand that the couple had confessed their affair while in a Bible study. The Lead Pastor had been afraid to confront the two leaders. But when the scandal broke (which it typically does eventually) it was terribly destructive to everyone involved. . How could this situation have been handled differently? How could the outcome have been less damaging for everyone involved? How do you think you would handle this situation?

This can be scary stuff, I know. It's better to be smart and never put yourself in a situation that would look terrible to someone looking in, or that you would have trouble defending. I would rather keep everyone as safe as possible and focus on the AMAZING work we get to do -every single week.

Landmine #2- Addiction

Between 17 percent and 30 percent of pastors admit to engaging in dangerous coping methods such as alcohol or other "substances" to manage ministry stress[21]. In my experience, there is no one more at risk for a serious addiction that someone who sincerely believes, "It can never happen to me." It is true that science has discovered a genetic link- a hereditary predisposition-to being an addict. However, in the right circumstances, or should I say the wrong circumstances?, anyone can become dependent on a substance or a behavior in their day to day life. What exactly is an "addiction?" Well, it is not just a "bad or annoying habit." The dictionary defines an **addiction** as: *" The state of being enslaved to a habit or practice or to something that is psychologically or* *physically habit-forming, as narcotics, to such an extent that its cessation causes severe trauma[8]."*

In other words, an addiction is a habit or practice that you become so completely dependent on, that it begins to interfere with your everyday life, and you have a decreased ability to function without it. What comes to mind when we think of the stereotypical "addict" is an alcoholic, or someone who is dependent on an illegal drug such as cocaine, heroin etc. But it is possible to become addicted to many things: legal/prescription medications, pornography, sex, television, food, gambling, shopping and more. The word "addiction" actually comes from the Latin, meaning "to give over to" "to surrender to." Addiction can start as something necessary for a time (prescription pain medications), but after too much time goes by, the brain and body literally change their chemistry, needing the drug just to "function." Sometimes an addiction starts as a recreational or social pastime-television, smoking, shopping. In many cases, the individual is using the substance or the behavior as a "coping mechanism" in order to deal with emotional or physical pain, stress, loss or illness. The coping mechanism releases feel good endorphins and stress releasing dopamine to counteract pain, stress etc. This is what the body and brain are supposed to do to get us through a SHORT time of "fight or flight."

---

[8] http://www.dictionary.com/browse/addiction

However, over time, the body releases less of these pleasant hormones or simply builds up a tolerance to them. Then the individual must drink more, smoke more, shop more etc. in order to get the same relief as they did before.[9]

Addiction is a major problem in the United States today. According to the United States Attorney General, 1 in 7 Americans will become addicted to a substance some time in their lives.[10]

As ministers, we deal with the terrible consequences of addiction all the time in our congregations- broken marriages, lost jobs, neglected children, destroyed lives...So how then could a pastor or strong Christian lay leader become addicted to something themselves?

I believe that pastors are at high risk for becoming addicts. They need to recognize that risk and guard against it. Pastors live in a relative state of high stress. We are at the side of those who are dying. We counsel families who are living through loss. We minister through tragedies. Our

---

[9] The National Institute on Drug Abuse Blog Team. (2017, January 12). Tolerance, Dependence, Addiction: What's the Difference?. Retrieved from https://teens.drugabuse.gov/blog/post/tolerance-dependence-addiction-whats-difference on June 26, 2019.

[10] https://www.usatoday.com/story/news/nation-now/2016/11/17/surgeon-general-1-7-us-face-substance-addiction/93993474/

work weeks are never 9-5, and they certainly do not stop when we get home. We are the sounding board for those who are hurting and suffering. We are counselors at times (which can be dangerous). We see and hear people at their worst. Ministry is at times a "sedentary profession," meaning that too many pastors do not get a lot of exercise. We do not often feel that we can be open with those around us about our stresses and fears, because we are "serving others." Most pastors do NOT have many friends they can talk to outside of their congregation. Too many leaders feel that they have failed it they go in to see a counselor. All of this together can be a recipe for disaster.

How many pastors pride themselves on never smoking or drinking, but they go for the "OK" addiction and binge eat-sometimes late at night or in secret? This often leads to diabetes, high cholesterol, heart disease and other medical problems.

How many leaders secretly spend too much money, running up way too much credit card debt in an attempt to ease stress? When they have a major financial crash, it can impact their credibility in handling the church's finances.

The news has been full lately of pastors who have lost their ministries because of an affair, sex addiction or pornography addiction. Many times this may start as a coping mechanism to deal with stress and emotional pain.

A saw a pastor on the news just a few weeks ago, that stepped down from a very large church/ministry that he had built due to an alcohol addiction that he could no longer hide. My heart broke for him and for his congregation. He is a caring, effective pastor, but he admitted that his secret coping method for all the enormous stress had gotten out of control. Another pastor I know, almost lost their ministry due to a secret addiction to prescription pain medications after a terrible car accident. I suspect the problem is much deeper than we know, because pastors are reluctant to reach out for help until the landmine explodes publicly (which it eventually does). The devastated congregation is usually grieving and bewildered, thinking, "How could our pastor have fallen like this?" But we need to remember that our pastors are human beings too who face incredible pain and stress. We often judge our Pastors more harshly than we would judge ourselves. This adds hurt upon hurt for the Pastor and his family.

Not all coping mechanisms are inherently "wrong." The Apostle Paul said it best in 1 Corinthians 6:12 when he said, "I will not be brought under the power of anything." Below is a list of possible ways to cope with the high stress of ministry, though this list is certainly NOT exhaustive.

Unacceptable Coping Methods- illegal drug use, pornography, adultery/fornication, violence, destroying things, threats, self harm, stealing, legal drug abuse, excessive spending etc.

Acceptable Coping Methods- (when not taken to extremes) exercise, talking to a friend, taking your days off weekly, taking your vacation days, having a weekly date night with your spouse, reading a great book, having a healthy hobby, listening to music, praying, going to a counselor (yes I mean it), going to a church service to be ministered to, gardening, journaling, eating WELL, sitting in the sun etc. etc.

A good pastor friend of mine adds, "I would strongly suggest requiring yourself to go to church with the congregation at least once a month if you serve in a capacity like a Children's Pastor where you do not get to go to church. If you go to church once a month, that's only twelve times a year! You may even find a Saturday service at a sister church to plug into.

If you feel that you are using ANY coping method to excess, or that you have lost or are at risk of losing control of your life to any substance or behavior, please get yourself to a professional counselor NOW. Learn how to deal with your stress and pain now. Do not let this landmine explode, perhaps destroying you, your marriage, your family, and/or your ministry. Realize that any of us are at risk and learn to manage the stress of ministry in a HEALTHY way. It is not too late. God is a God of restoration, healing and hope- not just for everyone else, but for us too. For more information on addiction, seeking help and finding acceptable coping strategies, check out:

https://addictionresource.com/

https://www.asam.org/resources/public-resources/resource-links

https://www.addictionguide.com/resources/

Landmine #3- Mishandling of Church Money

"But Trish, you just don't understand. The people in our finance office are always after me to turn in my receipts for church expenses, and to fill out paperwork for reimbursement! Then they want to know specifics about what exactly the money was used for and why. It's like they don't believe me. And that hurts! I mean, I'm a LEADER in this ministry! I'm sacrificing here to make this happen. Sometimes I get so irritated by all of their questions that I just pay for it myself rather than deal with the paperwork. I shouldn't have to explain why I need this or what I'm going to do with it. I signed up to work with people; I don't want to explain myself and every purchase. And I'm a minister- not a finance person. So what if I can't find some of the receipts, or a paper or two? They are

nitpicking, which means they don't care about this ministry. Why can't the finance people be supportive of the kid's/youth/family/outreach ministry? It's like they keep us from getting ministry done. I've been at this church for _____ years. They should just trust me! **Why can't they just trust me***?"*

I have heard this argument so many times over the years from frustrated ministry leaders. It is almost a cliché, and a joke at pastor's meetings. We believe that creative, absent minded ministry leaders are going to butt heads repeatedly with the logical, calculating finance people. And I do want to say, I fully understand that there needs to be balance. The ministry leader needs to feel appreciated, respected and valued; AND they need to have a voice at the table that makes those financial decisions. Using your church's children's ministry department as an example, children should make up at least 25 percent of your church body as a whole, which impacts all those parents and all those volunteers etc. Anyone with that much influence should have a VERY large portion of the church's overall budget, AND a strong voice when it comes to making financial decisions that impact the church and/or the kid's ministry.

Having said that, however, I want to pause for a moment and say emphatically: Dear church leader, **NO they should NOT just trust you**. And you need to see those finance people at your church as allies and safeguards for you, and work VERY hard not to be a source of frustration for them. And here are a few reasons why:

1.There are relatively few failures in ministry that have the potential to destroy you, your family and your entire ministry, now and possibly for life. The first of course is a sexual fall. But secondly, right behind that, is a conviction for mishandling, misappropriating MONEY. What has taken down so many Pastors, ministers, televangelists and missions' organizations in the past decade? Mishandling money includes embezzlement, putting funds to an area illegally, not paying appropriate fees, false advertising while fundraising etc. Many charities reported a net loss of income last year and attributed it to "lack of trust" from the public to religious organizations, after so many money scandals have hit the news. Churches MUST be more responsible.

2.Those finance people are also there to protect YOU and that ministry. We already said that one scandal can forever mar your ministry. But sometimes all it takes is someone getting irritated with you and making *accusations* that cast doubt in people's minds. During those times, and if you are ever formally accused of mishandling money, those finance people are your saving grace and your very best friend. And you will thank God on your knees for every receipt you turned in to prove exactly where that money went. When I worked as a security trainer, we had a rule, "If it isn't in writing, it didn't happen." What that means is, it is too late after the fact, when you are already in hot water to try to figure out which money went where. One of the KEY functions of your church's finance officer, and board is to keep great WRITTEN records- every form, every receipt, and every budget request. Please understand this: "ONLY WHAT IS IN WRITING IS GOING TO COUNT." If anything ever did go to court, or a serious accusation is made, no one is just going to just "trust you." And your word on it is going to mean next to nothing. Those receipts, and those records will either be your saving grace or your downfall. DON'T fight your finance office on keeping careful records. Learn to understand and appreciate them.

3.Everyone needs accountability. EVERYONE. Even a pastor. And whenever someone continually resists being accountable, it begins to look suspicious. Too many awful moral failures have happened because leaders refused to be accountable to anyone. That is not Biblical. And they shouldn't have to chase you down and force you to be accountable. You should be willingly open to Biblical accountability- and MONEY is a huge part of that. Be accountable. Some churches I know make it a policy that it takes two signers on any church check, or that whenever the church credit card is used, the finance director gets a report. This is an example of willing accountability. Nothing done with the church money should ever be done with only one person's knowledge. Nothing should be done without a paper trail. No one should have to sneak around to act with church money. If these things are going on, something is very wrong, and it will come back around to bite you.

4.This is people's tithe money/sacrificial giving. This is even more important that someone's 401K, to God. This is people's hard earned, faith given, oft times SACRIFICIAL giving. And no one in church leadership should ever take that huge responsibility lightly. Every single cent needs to be accounted for, and used with wisdom for God's kingdom. God holds His ministers to a higher standard. So we should be extremely careful to be good stewards of God's money- people's TITHE AND OFFERING money.

5.You are responsible to explain what you need for ministry to the leadership of the church. Even if you say, "but I just wanted to be with the kids," part of your job of the ministry leader is to accurately and effectively communicate to the church's leadership, what your ministry needs to be successful. And that will entail giving some rationale. That means you will have to explain often in writing presented at a board meeting some things like, "What JumpStart3? Why I feel we should get it? What it costs? This is why I chose it over _____." Your board is not in your area of ministry every week. You have to assume they have no IDEA what the difference is between a PVC puppet stage and an aluminum travel stage. You will need to do your homework. Make a good case for what you need. And if they say no, graciously accept it and don't burn bridges. Don't gossip and don't pout. Wait, pray, and keep track of your numbers- Board meetings typically occur monthly so there is another opportunity to talk about this. Build a better case and try again. If you are asked to explain WHY you need such a curriculum, be grateful! Grateful that you have the chance to talk about the ministry and vision cast to a portion of the congregation who may not know what God has been doing. That's why they hired you. . It's your chance to speak up and connect!

I cannot say it is easy. You may feel like you're always defending the ministry God has called you to and that you're not being trusted. But please know, those financial safeguards are there for a reason. Maybe this week would be a good week to bring your financial officer an extra large apple cider- and turn in your receipts. Yes, it is that serious. It is not optional for churches to have safeguards in place. Scandals destroy lives, churches, ministries- and worse, they drag the name of Jesus and Christianity right through the mud on every news channel. These scandals LINGER in people's minds for years to come. We are called to be the watchmen of the integrity of the church. A high calling indeed!

AND NOW: A modern day parable...

"Well, Ms. Churches, I have your test results here, and the good news is we do know the reason why you have such a terrible earache," said the doctor, shutting the door behind him. He pushed his glasses up with his forefinger and shifted his stare from his clipboard to the middle of her face.

"Oh, that's a relief!" she breathed impatiently. "Can you write me a prescription for that so I can get going? I'm in the middle of some very important work! So if you could just...."

"Ms. Churches, I need your full attention here for a minute. The bad news I have for you is that the earache is not the real problem here. The tests results confirmed what I suspected the moment you walked in here. Your earache is, of course, related to that enormous tumor- right there in the middle of your face. I have to ask, are you currently in treatment for that?"

"Oh THIS? I'm sure this really isn't THAT serious. And I do not consider myself a negative person. I do not allow negativity in my life. And I do not appreciate your complaining and negativity either."

"Ms. Churches, I am not being negative. Negative comments about the tumor would be- 'That's ugly, it's horrible, Who's fault is the tumor? Who can we blame? I hate the person who has the tumor! It's hopeless! Let's give up! ' Ms. Churches, I am not saying any of those things. But you DO have a very large facial tumor. And it IS serious. What I AM saying is, 'Let's realize how serious this is and come up with a plan to get rid of this tumor before it hurts you anymore.'"

"Doctor H.S. , I just don't have time for this right now. I am helping a lot of people with my work! Haven't you seen the signs all over town? Ms. Church is helping more than ever'? What would happen if people found out I had a face tumor? It might detract from all the good I'm trying to do. And I'm planning a wedding! I can't have a facial surgery right now- I'd have scars. You just haven't seen me with all my makeup on. I'm really good at hiding all this with my makeup."

"Don't you understand that you cannot go on hiding something rotten and cancerous forever? The One you Love will want you to be healthy, scars and all. That thing is killing you, and parts of you are getting hurt that shouldn't have to get hurt. Every day you let this go, your body is not operating like it should. Eventually the tumor will spread everywhere and take over. All the good you are trying to do for everyone will come to an end. If you do not address and kill the cancer, it will kill you. Please face this! Better to go through the pain and recovery now- FACE THIS."

"You physicians think you are so great! You just don't understand at all. It's not my place to go meddling with nature like that. If God wants to step in and fix it eventually He will. I'll just wait on Him-"

"I'm just gonna cut you off right there. God gave us intelligence for a reason. He entrusted us with these bodies, and we are the ones who are supposed to manage our health for Him. When something isn't healthy, we must work to make it right again. Be a better steward of what He gave you Ms. Churches."

"Ok, you want the truth? I'm just afraid. I'm afraid of what will happen when we see how bad the damage is. How deep does it go?. How much is going to have to be cut away? How long will it take to get back on the road to health again...I'm afraid of admitting all this and doing the hard work."

"So many die every year because they were too afraid to face reality, and fight the cancer when it was still small enough to remove. The real fear should be waiting too long, of good healthy qualities being destroyed. I know you are afraid. But will you take my hand and talk with me about options to destroy this tumor for good? No more denying it, hiding it, talking nice about it, excusing it or covering it up? You can still get healthy before your wedding. Are you willing to fight for that?"

Chapter 8- Anxiety, Depression and.....Ministry??

The audience seemed to hold its collective breath. The lady next to me put her pencil down on her planner. Many heads came up to see if they were hearing her right. To be sure, Christine Yount Jones had everyone's full attention. You see, Christine, a respected kid's ministry voice for most of her life, was a keynote speaker at this past January's CPC (Children's Pastors Conference). And Christine had just broached the subject of anxiety, depression and the ministry leader. With thoughtfulness, humor and raw honesty, she validated a lot of people there that day; talking about the different ways that God "calms the storm" in our lives.

After I got home, I noticed a conversation on a popular ministry forum, possibly sparked by this session. A staff pastor shared that she battled with depression, but that God was giving her the energy and strength every week to minister effectively to families. Her comment seemed to break an unseen barrier as more and more leaders began sharing their stories as well. One leader, an older man, shared that he had felt like a failure after going in for counseling after a particularly rough church transition. But he discovered that this counseling was the best decision EVER for him, and for his family and his ministry. Yet another pastor said how tough it can be to fight through your own battles to minister to others who are in need. How many of us HIDE it from others-especially at our church-when we are anxious, depressed or hurting? Do we feel like "lesser" ministers when we are depressed? Can God use us through our own pain to help others?

I highly recommend reading this article from churchleaders.com:

https://churchleaders.com/pastors/pastor-articles/144651-silent-suffering-pastors-and-depression.html. It includes among other facts:

"The likelihood is that one out of every four pastors is depressed," said *Matthew Stanford, a professor of psychology and neuroscience at Baylor University in Waco, Texas. But anxiety and depression in the pulpit are "markedly higher" in the last five years, said Fred Smoot, executive director of Emory Clergy Care in Duluth, Georgia.*

Nearly two out of three depressed people don't seek treatment, according to studies by the Depression and Bipolar Support Alliance. Counselors say even fewer depressed ministers get treated because of career fears, social stigma and spiritual taboo. Matthew Stanford, a professor of psychology and neuroscience at Baylor University in Waco, Texas, who studies how the Christian community deals with mental illness, said depression in Christian culture carries "a double stigmatization." He explains that Society still places a stigma on mental illness, but Christians make it worse, he said, by "over-spiritualizing depression and other disorders—dismissing them as a lack of faith or a sign of weakness."

After a lot of prayer, I felt I needed to include this chapter, because some of my fellow ministry leaders and fellow believers may need this word. Here are some things I really want you to know:

1.Anxiety and Depression are mood disorders- they do NOT disqualify you from ministry any more than having diabetes or a thyroid disorder would. Some of the most talented, creative pastors I know battle bipolar disorder or anxiety.

2.So many suffer in the shadows. Sometimes you might think you are the only one. You are not! People are not always as sunny and perfect as their social media profiles lead you to believe! We really do not know someone else's daily struggles.

3.God understands- He really does, and He cares. God wants to ease our anxiety and our depression. Did you know that there are over 500 Scriptures in the Bible about dealing with fear (anxiety)?? We wouldn't need all of those promises from God if Christians got a free pass for no anxiety or sadness. We are never promised a life free of pain this side of heaven. See below for some of my favorite verses for anxiety, sadness or confusion. We need to remember that Jesus understands. He is acquainted with our sorrow. He was fully human as well as fully God. He even said, speaking of His soon approaching death, "I have a baptism to be baptized with (the Crucifixion), and how ANXIOUS I am until it is accomplished!" (Luke 12:50, emphasis mine). In the Garden of Gethsemane He said, "My soul is overwhelmed with sorrow even unto death!" (Mark 14:34). He understands! And He hears and acts to help.

4.A counselor is rarely a poor decision. Who would ever shame a diabetic for talking with their doctor?? But for the ministry leader who is focused on helping everyone else- getting help can be the hardest part. A word of wisdom...It would be foolish to trust everyone around you with all of your private battles. You need someone safe that you can talk to openly. I went in for professional counseling several years ago, as I struggled to get over a devastating loss. As tough as that was, it was such a great decision. I needed to heal in order to keep giving out in ministry to others.

5.Ministry has the capacity to make us prone to depression. I know what we deal with on a weekly basis can be overwhelming, and often misunderstood. People are hurting and broken. We ministers love others through the fallout of deaths, sexual assaults, broken marriages, abused children, suicides, car accidents and so much more. Ministry is not a nine to five job; it is your whole life a lot of times! It consumes your whole heart and soul! That is why we have to be on our guard to minister to our OWN soul. Pastors are notorious for not taking their days off, or their vacation days. We work WAY too many hours. How's your soul? How is our relationship with Jesus? Yes, self-care matters.

6.God created you, He loves you and His plan for your life is not over because of what you are going through. As Paul said, "His strength is made perfect in our weakness." Yes, God can and will use you, in your brokenness. But He also cares about YOUR health and joy.

A few weeks ago, a well known pastor of a very large church in my area took his own life. At the time of this writing, the whole city, as well as his family and his congregation, are reeling from the loss. He helped so many people, including some who were depressed themselves. What are the signs that you or someone you love may be suicidal[11]? Do any of these scenarios apply to you?

- Giving away possessions, even those that had been held dear
- Having thoughts like, "My family would be better without me…"
- Talking about suicide, hurting yourself, death, or dying
- Seeking access to firearms or pills
- Withdrawing from friends, family, and society
- Having severe mood swings
- Feeling hopeless or trapped
- Increased use of alcohol or drugs

---

[11] Sitzes, Jenae. "Suicide Prevention: How to Spot the Signs of Suicide." *Www.prevention.com*, September 28, 2018. Accessed June 29, 2019. https://www.prevention.com/health/mental-health/a21234585/signs-suicide-prevention/.

- Sleeping all the time or having issues with sleep

- Uncontrolled rage or agitation

- Self-destructive and risky behavior

- Telling people goodbye for seemingly no reason

- A major change in everyday behavior

If you said "yes" to one or more of the above warning signs, it may be time to ask for help. Can I just say, if you are feeling down or overwhelmed, please do not harm yourself. Do not be embarrassed to go in for help. Many people love you and would be so lost without you. If you were asking God to speak, maybe this is Him speaking into your life saying, "*I love you. It IS going to be OK. I do have an amazing plan for your life. You are not a failure, you're My special creation. Hang on, this WILL get better.*"

National Suicide Prevention Hotline (24 hours) Call 1-800-273-8255

A few of Trisha's favorite verses to read in time of anxiety and/or sadness:

So do not fear, for I am with you;
   do not be dismayed, for I am your God.
I will strengthen you and help you;
   I will uphold you with my righteous right hand. (Isaiah 41:10).
Why are you in despair, O my soul? And why are you disturbed within me? Hope in God, for I shall again praise Him, The help of my countenance and my God. (Psalm 43:5).

But when I am afraid, I will put my confidence in you. Yes, I will trust the promises of God. And since I am trusting him, what can mere man do to me? (Psalm 56:3-4)

For I know the plans I have for you," declares the Lord, "plans to prosper you and not to harm you, plans to give you hope and a future. (Jeremiah 29:11).

I remain confident of this: I will see the goodness of the LORD in the land of the living. (Psalm 27:13).

Chapter 9- From Burnout to Blowout to Timeout

Should I take Monday? Should I take Friday? Will I EVER get a day off?

Ministers need a strong commitment to physical and mental health, exercise, healthy eating, seeing the doctor regularly, sleeping, and taking vacations. Self-care needs to become a habit. Pastors who have survived burnout and have bounced back highly recommend taking sabbaticals and other times away to reflect and recover[12].
Finding a way to limit the enmeshment and put strong boundaries in place between church and home is crucial. This is part and parcel of reassessing priorities and committing to better time management. A pastor's marriage and family have to have quality and quantity of time.

Job satisfaction, a feeling of being successful, of having control and having choices is so important to avoiding burnout. Burnout can come with a feeling of powerlessness and failure. Ministers who had a strong internal sense of their own goals, their own calling and their own "merits" did much better in fighting off depression and burnout[13]. Those who adhered to external criteria for success, such as congregants' expectations, tended to become frustrated and hopeless over time[14].

---

[12] Fallon, Barry, Simon Rice, and Joan Wright Howie. *"Factors That Precipitate and Mitigate Crises in Ministry."* Pastoral Psychology62, no. 1 (2012): 27-40. doi:10.1007/s11089-012-0486-4.

[13] Palmer. *Let Your Life Speak. Listening for the Voice of Vocation.* John Wiley & Sons, Incorporated, 2009.

Fighting burnout effectively means realizing you are not powerless, and taking control over your schedule.

If you are like me, with a combination of travel, leadership and parenting it may feel IMPOSSIBLE to take a day off. But I want to tell you right now, it is imperative that you DO take a day off each week and that you make that day off as effective as possible, and here's how:

1. First of all, _you have to believe that it IS possible to take a day off_. Too many ministers and leaders and parents have given into the lie of our modern culture that it is not possible, or wise to take a day off. The lie says, "You MUST be a GOOD worker, and a GOOD parent, and to be a GOOD worker and a GOOD parent you must ....(work 80 hours, take the kids to soccer, hockey, ballet, karate, speech meets, playmates, etc). What we really need to do is separate cultural expectations from what scripture actually says. We really do not need to work that many hours. We do not need to please that many people. We do not need to have our children in that many activities. It's time to kill the martyr complex. If you absolutely cannot find one day to take off for yourself, than some activities will have to be cut. If some people are disappointed, then that is ok. You are not on earth to please everyone. You are on earth to glorify God and to please Him. **God tells us to take one day in seven to**

[14] Doolittle, Benjamin R. "_The Impact of Behaviors upon Burnout Among Parish-Based Clergy._" Journal of Religion and Health49, no. 1 (2008): 88-95. doi:10.1007/s10943-008-9217-7.

rest; therefore it IS possible to do it. If we feel we cannot take one day in seven to rest, we are doing too much to please other humans instead of God. If pastors of massive churches have found ways to be faithful in resting before God, you can to. With a husband, five services a week, two small children, traveling, five employees, an intern, a more than full time schedule and a partridge in a pear tree, I have made a way to have a day off almost every week (emergencies do happen), but it was WORK to make that happen. But first, I had to believe it was the right thing to do, and that it was possible to have a day off every week. For parents, I used to think I couldn't ever have a day or even an evening to myself. I told a friend, "I cannot afford a sitter right now." She said, "Will someone watch your children for free so you can have a day off?" I said, "No one would ever do that." She said simply, "Have you ever asked?" I was stunned to silence. I did start asking and very soon a kind lady from our church said yes. And I finally had "time off" each week.

2. You are going to have to plan and work toward having your day off or your vacation time off with the same creativity as any other event on your calendar. Did you just yell unfair? That may well be unfair. But if you do not work to plan and protect your day off, other things will creep in and steal it away. What do I mean by plan and protect your day off? I do not schedule anything on my day off. Not dentist visits or doctor's checkups. Not teacher meetings. If people from church ask to meet that day, I respond, "I cannot, because I have something scheduled that day.

How about the day after?" I do not say, "That's my day off," because people are shockingly flippant about days off, saying "oh, then I'll just come by your house and we can meet there!" I will deliberately plan to be out of town in a state park on my day off where there is no cell signal.

You are NOT powerless as far as your schedule goes; you have more control than you think!

When someone says, "we are doing _____ on (your day off)" many times you CAN say, "No, I can't that day. I have a commitment. How about _____?" It's a lot of work, but it's worth it. And what if it is your senior leader or someone on your staff who regularly disrespects your day off? You may have inadvertently trained this person that your day off didn't matter. And you can retrain them that now your day off DOES matter. It takes time and patience and good communication. "I would rather not do our outreach debrief on our day off if at all possible. I had planned to take my family to the zoo that day. We could all use a day of break after that big weekend. Could we all meet _____?" Be respectful, but start making a case your time OFF to be time OFF. If your senior leader does not honor their own time off, they probably will not honor yours either. But YOU need to keep working toward a day of rest for the sake of your relationship with God, your spouse and your family anyway. Put your days off on the calendar at home and at church and protect them at all costs. Put your out of office reply on and let your voicemail pick up. That's what it is for.

3. Remember your reasons for taking a day of rest. God told us to do so all throughout the Bible. He set the example for us in Scripture. The burnout rates of ministers are high because ministers tend to be the LEAST obedient to God about taking a day off! You are not doing ANYBODY any good if you burn out and leave ministry. Your family needs you. And you get only one chance to make memories with the family God gave you. You will be a better minister if you take a day off once a week. Your relationship with God will be better and closer if you are obedient to Him to rest once a week. "Obedience is better than sacrifice." We really like to be in charge. But our ministry can dramatically change for the better when we decide to be obedient and rest in Him. Your health depends on learning to rest. You'll do ministry for the Lord longer on this earth if you learn to take days off! So ***stop flinging yourself off cliffs and demanding that angels catch you as you crash and fry yourself!***

4. Plan activities for your day off that will refill and renew YOU. Do not just hope that your day off will "happen." You may just end up folding clothes and raking and then wonder why you're still tired at work the next day. What energizes you? What makes you feel new again? It is not

the same for all of us. For introverts, it is usually time alone, away from it all. If that's you, maybe you should schedule some hiking time for yourself, or time on a secluded beach, a nap with all phones and lights off etc. Extroverts, like myself, get energy from being around people! I refill from going to a movie (phone off) or the mall with friends or the zoo with my family. I do not like staying around my house because 9 times out of 10 I end of doing housework or someone from church finds me with a minor crisis. No matter what it is, find out what refuels you, and then schedule THAT on your day off- NOT things for work, or house work, or school work- nothing that DRAINS you. I know this is difficult. It is a discipline but it is worth it.

VACATIONS: Did you know that Americans, on average, are TERRIBLE about not taking their vacation days[15]? God has given us physical and emotional boundaries that He wants each human to respect. When a pastor does not respect these boundaries, by overworking, eating poorly, and not resting, it grieves God. However, God will not violate the pastor's boundaries. God will allow the pastor to feel the consequences of his or her lack of boundaries. The ensuing illness and exhaustion is supposed to teach us to better respect the limits God gave us. Ministers need a strong commitment to physical and mental health, exercise, healthy eating, seeing the doctor regularly, sleeping, and taking

[15] Ashford, Kate. "Why Americans Aren't Taking Half Of Their Vacation Days." Forbes. June 01, 2017.

vacations. For several years now, Americans have been taking fewer and fewer days off each year. "In 2016, 54% of employees ended the year with unused time off, collectively sacrificing 662 million vacation days," according to a study the U.S. Travel Association's Project Time Off. This problem of not taking vacation days, is probably even worse in the church. Too many pastors report feeling apprehensive to go on vacation. One pastor's wife explains, "It seems like the second we are out of the city limits something disastrous happens. Every single time! Three years ago, we had just arrived at our destination for our yearly vacation when we received an emergency phone call telling us that the elderly assistant pastor from our church had slipped and fallen on the ice near his home. He hit his head so hard that he passed away just hours later. His family only wanted us to do the funeral. This year, before we could even reach our hotel, the youth pastor called us to let us know that four families had gotten into an argument over a Wednesday night kid's ministry program and now all four families were leaving the church! Again, our trip was ruined. Now my husband never wants to leave town on vacation for fear of another blow up."

4. To minister effectively, you are going to have to keep adapting. We've all met them. Ministers who learned something in Bible College or on a missions trip 25 years ago- and they haven't changed their approach or methods since. They thought they learned, "how it's done" and to this day, they just do those outdated things over and over again, even

without getting any results. They do not know any other way and are unwilling to learn new ways. The message of salvation in Jesus Christ does not change- but our methods for reaching this generation can and will. We must continually keep training and learning to keep up. Otherwise our ministry becomes the equivalent of moving to Shanghai, screaming your sermon at the people in Swahili, and then condemning them all for "not being interested or engaged." Of course they aren't listening! You aren't speaking their language! About every 10-15 years, the "language" we speak here in the United States changes drastically. If you aren't growing and changing with it, you are wasting your time and theirs, preaching words that are not having the desired effect. Paul said, "I have become all things to all men, that by any means I may save some." (1 Cor. 9:22) Want to be an effective leader? Learn the language and culture of the people God has sent you to. Learn some new methods of doing ministry. Change up those cultural references and object lessons. You don't have to be 'hip'. You just have to be willing to love people and meet them where they are. Let's never be too stubborn or lazy to learn what we have to, to reach whomever we can. Jesus died to reach those people- and now He has called you to tell them about His love and His offer of a new life. There is no greater message or responsibility on earth! Let's tell His message often, clearly and in as many ways as possible!

So I hope you can see, the best hope for a better church, is a better YOU. Start with what you have- yourself! What steps can you take right NOW to improve yourself as a leader and to prepare for whatever God has for your next? It's an exciting adventure...one that's just getting started...Ministry is not a short sprint (though there are sprinting seasons). Ministry is a grueling marathon. And it is worth it! "Therefore run with endurance the race that is set before you. Throw off the sin that so easily trips you up...." Hebrews 12:1.

I know how difficult it is to get a day off or a vacation week off, and sometimes life happens, so it just does not work out. But that should be the exception, not the rule. I just wanna encourage you today and give you hope that you and your family are WORTH having that day off every week. It's Biblical and it's what's best for you, your family, your staff, and your church and ministry! Taking a break is a lot of work, so let's get to it-

Hang in There

Let's face it: Longevity matters. Long term relationships matter. Yes, sometimes God does call us to leave, but make sure it's really His time. Don't ever be quick too run. You are not alone. We all have those moments when we are tempted to throw in the towel, but the greatest payoffs and sweetest rewards come to those who put in the hard work over time. Don't quit. Don't give up. The same God Who called you, will equip you, not just for today, but for tomorrow and for all the many days ahead.

Therefore we do not lose heart...For momentary, light affliction is producing for us an eternal weight of glory far beyond all comparison." 2 Corinthians 4:16-18 (NASB)

Therefore, since we have so great a cloud of witnesses surrounding us, let us also lay aside every encumbrance and... run with endurance the race that is set before us." • Hebrews 12:1 (NASB)

ABOUT THE AUTHOR:

"Pastor Trisha Peach- For over 20 years, Pastor Trisha has been partnering with kids and families to create cutting edge kids' and family ministries. Her motto is: Nothing matters more than reaching this next generation for Jesus- so let's make an IMPACT that will last! Pastor Trisha shares her life and ministry with her husband Scott and their two children Logan and Eliana. Pastor Trish is an ordained minister with a passion to empower and encourage other children's ministers in their efforts to reach these precious kids and families for Jesus."

CAN'T GET ENOUGH PEACH?

Check out Trisha's weekly practical ministry show on YouTube "The Peach Buzz." Like and Subscribe today!

Follow her blog "PeachT" on Wordpress- http://peacht.wordpress.com

See her travel and speaking schedule, schedule her to come to your church at www.kidmin.ninja

Follow her on social media!
Www.facebook.com/pastortrisha
Www.Twitter.com/ptrishapeach

Explore her other 2 books, "Your Children's Ministry From Scratch," and "Your Children's Ministry Beyond Basics," available on Amazon, Kindle, Barnes and Noble and others

Made in the USA
Columbia, SC
04 November 2019